PARADES, PARTIES, AND PROTESTS
CREATIVE RESISTANCE CULTURE
BY SARAH SPARKLES

2ND EDITION

ISBN-13: 978-0-9883997-3-0

PARADES, PARTIES, AND PROTESTS

CREATIVE RESISTANCE CULTURE

ESSAYS AND PHOTOGRAPHY
BY SARAH SPARKLES

TABLE OF CONTENTS

INTRODUCTION

In the fall of 2000, the Supreme Court appointed George W. Bush president of the United States of America after he lost the election by 543,895 popular votes (FEC, 2001). The 2000 election was the first in which I was eligible to participate. I was devastated that the U.S. inaugurated a president that had not been legitimately elected, and who did not represent me. A year later, on September 11th, 2001, while many Americans watched the World Trade Center attack on television, I watched it from my kitchen window. Perched on my fire escape in Queens, I witnessed the flames and massive clouds of debris billowing from the Twin Towers. Within an hour, all that was left was smoke... and the world as I knew it had changed forever.

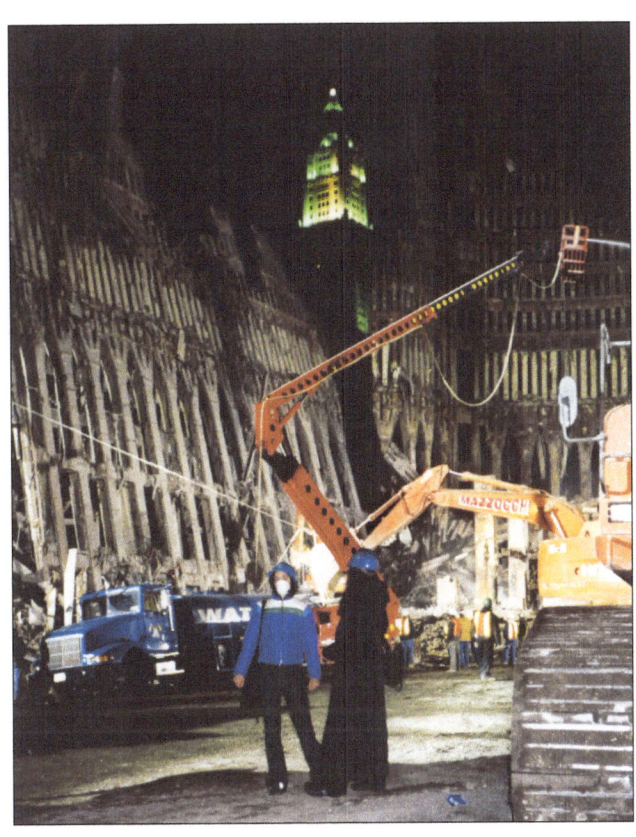

Ground Zero, September 2001

The catastrophic attacks that were unleashed upon New York City, Pennsylvania, and Washington D.C. on September 11th catalyzed one of the most critical turning points in American history. The Bush administration declared preemptive war (ironically entitled the "War on Terror") on any individual, collective or nation deemed a threat to national security. This would come to include Iraq, Afghanistan, and Pakistan, as well as immigrants, artists, and activists in America. My college years were molded by apprehension of war, terrorism, and the government. In the years following 9/11, the U.S. endured a dramatic escalation of domestic surveillance, two ongoing wars, a tanking economy, and a formidable loss of credibility within the international community. Against this nebulous backdrop of a democratic society in decline, a dynamic culture of hope and renewal was born as millions of people participated in protests that responded creatively to the turmoil of the times. Despite extreme restrictions placed on venues, public spaces and media outlets, the innovative culture of resistance that emerged inspired me to write a bold chronicle that pays tribute to this pivotal moment in history.

Parades, Parties, and Protests is a photo-journalistic account of the cultural aftermath of 9/11 witnessed from the perspective of my immersion in under-represented grassroots artist and activist communities in New York City and beyond. Aimed at confronting a decade of mass media hegemony, this book serves as both a testament and tool for anyone, anywhere who adamantly opposed the Bush administration, the Iraq war, and the on-going erosion of public space and civil liberties. The revolutionary subcultures featured in this book strive to manifest uplifting societal change by using art as a social critique, a medium for healing, and a political tool. The grassroots artist communities and protest movements of the 21st century embody a resourceful "do-it-yourself" culture that thrives on producing unique media and cultural events as a platform for education, entertainment, spirituality, and social justice. These movements embrace creativity as vital life force energy, uphold the sanctity of freedom of expression and assembly, champion the need for collective social spaces, and call for a humane paradigm to replace exploitative capitalist systems.

Parades, Parties, and Protests explores the interconnected relationship between corporations, mass media, and the government, in order to expose the injustices that have spawned many contemporary dissent movements. The theoretical framework of this book is derived from Karl Marx's and Friedrich Engel's influential writing *The Ruling Class, and the Ruling Ideas* (Marx and Engels, 2001), Italian Marxist Antonio Gramsci's concept of hegemony (Storey, 2003), and German researcher Max Horkheimer's investigation of the culture industry (Horkheimer and Adorno, 1995). One of the keynotes of the Marxist school of thought was that the upper echelon owns the means of production of mass media and consumer goods, and therefore exerts all pervasive control by shaping the intellectual framework and social mores of a society. This principle correlates with the current social landscape in which corporate conglomerates dominate ownership of mass media outlets and promote a voracious consumer culture, one that perpetuates their lordship. This results in the insidious neglect of pressing social and environmental concerns, and the flagrant misrepresentation of alternative subcultures and protest movements. *Parades, Parties, and Protests* also probes the Bush administration's questionable motives for initiating the Iraq War. It includes an investigation of the administration's conflicts of interest with the oil and weapons industry and the origins of the preemptive war doctrine formulated in the early 1990's by the neo-con think tank Project for a New American Century. The outrageous premise on which the Iraq War was launched in March 2003 inspired the largest anti-war protest movement in history.

In the 21st century, acts of dissent are more diverse than ever before, and with the revolutionary innovations in high-speed multimedia communication technology there is a greater capability of reaching a global audience. Traditional forms of activism such as marches and petitions are now widely accompanied by online social media campaigns, avant-garde protests staged as parodies, non-permitted public celebrations, and art festivals in remote locations. The most prominent styles of protest utilized in post-9/11 America are categorized here as Agitprop, Witness, and Utopia. Many of the most inspirational events at this time were a fusion of these dynamic mediums. "Agitprop" is an art-based framework for activism that incorporates performance, puppetry, costuming, and signage to communicate a political message to a diverse audience. "Witness" demonstrations take the form of memorials and effigies within a social setting. They mourn tragedy, provide representation for the marginalized, and illuminate critical social concerns that may be nearly impossible to eradicate, but must nevertheless must be acknowledged. "Utopian" events provide a variety of open forums for expression, spontaneous interaction, and community-building in environments that offer minimal commerce. These unique cultural gatherings challenge an existing social order as participants cultivate alternative paradigms that reflect a more ideal world.

Parades, Parties, and Protests documents a vibrant, ephemeral culture where the majority of events took place in public spaces or at venues that no longer exist. In the face of an ever-changing landscape, I embarked on a decade-long exploration of inspirational cultural happenings; public processions around New York City, multimedia events that combined art and activism, all-night dance parties in warehouses, and pilgrimages to festivals in remote parts of the country. These alternative gatherings fostered a platform for art that is therapeutic and cathartic, being developed in communities that are under constant threat of extinction. At a time when many alternative voices were shut out of the mass media, these dynamic grassroots events became a driving force for disseminating information and cultivating an uplifting transformative culture. In the face of adversity, people from around the world came together, daring to create the world they dreamed to live in. This is their story.

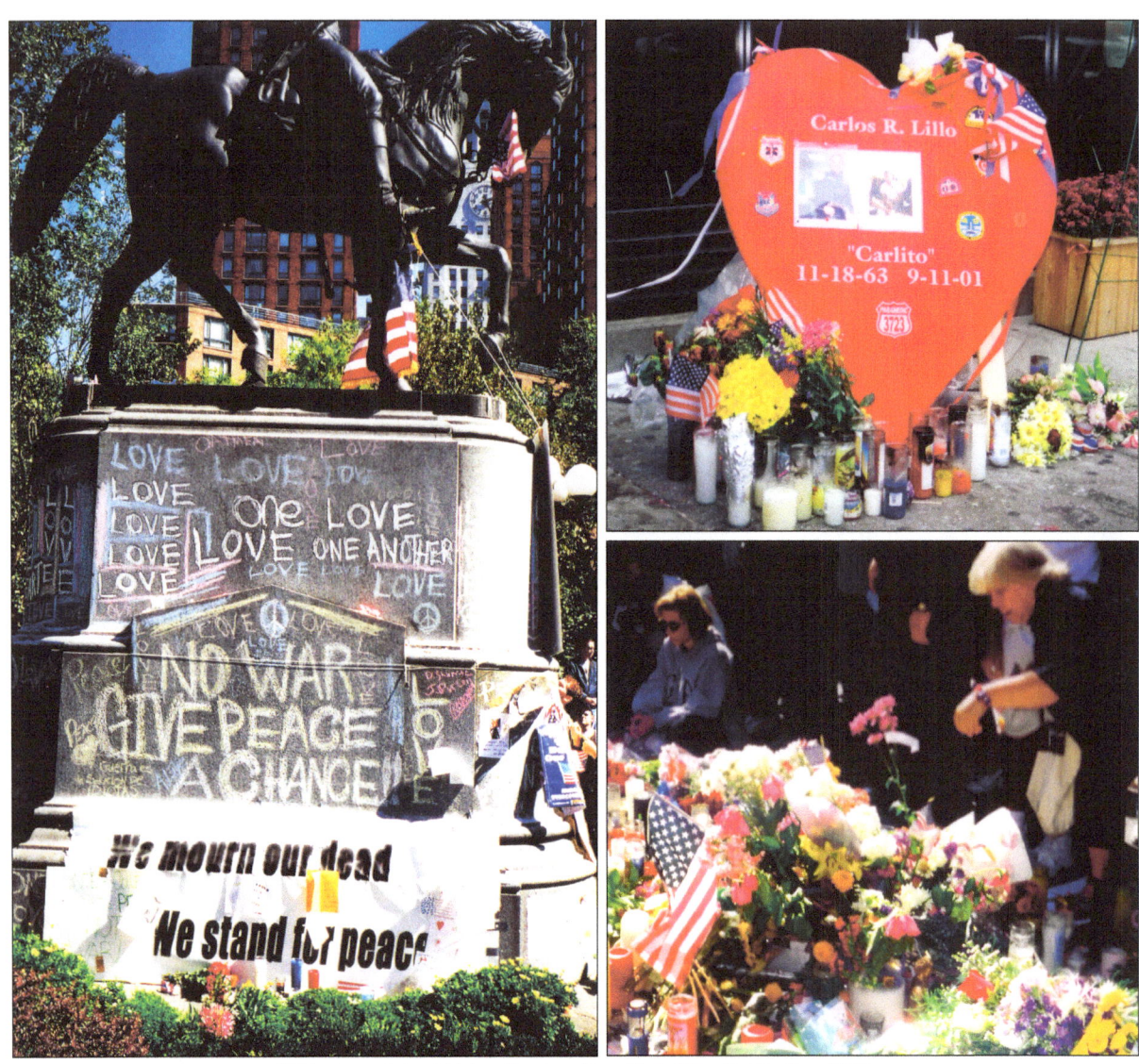

9/11 memorials at Union Square, New York City, September 2001

“ **WE MOURN OUR DEAD.**
WE STAND FOR PEACE. ”

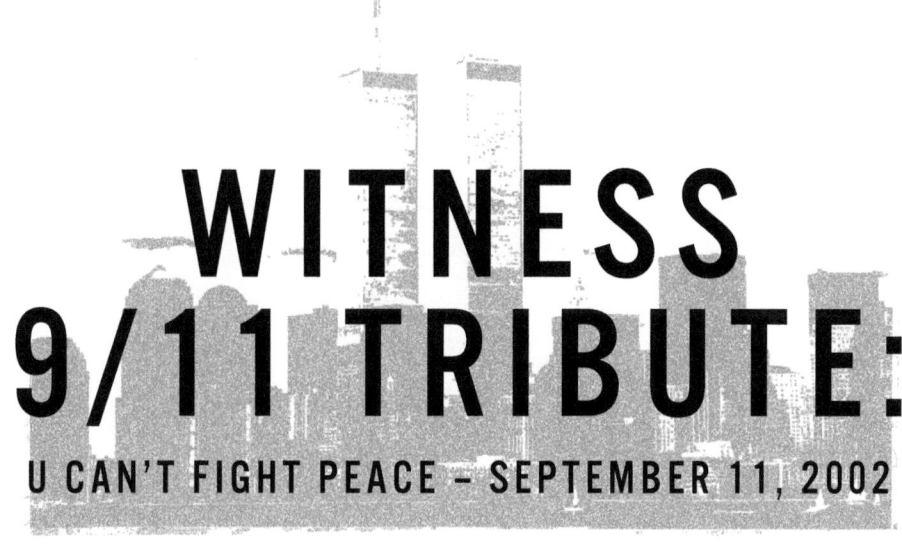

WITNESS 9/11 TRIBUTE:
U CAN'T FIGHT PEACE – SEPTEMBER 11, 2002

In the days that followed the terrorist attacks on September 11th, 2001, New York City found itself in an impenetrable state of mourning. Collages of missing person ads, candle-lit vigils, and shrines paying homage to the dead marked every corner of the city. Everyone had a story about where they were when the planes crashed, who they had known who'd worked in the towers, and the ever-present gaping hole in the skyline. Eventually the dust settled, and as the weeks and months passed the city returned to business as usual. The street vendors stopped selling American flags and resumed selling fake Gucci and Prada. The air down by Ground Zero was deemed safe. The candles burnt out and the weathered memorials faded. However, the impact of 9/11 was a monumental loss that unfolded over time. For some it was the loss of loved ones coupled with the loss of an innate sense of security. For others it was the loss of New York City's rugged effervescence and of civil liberties for which they had never questioned entitlement.

A culture of fear emerged in the years following 9/11. Surveillance, intrusion, and encroachment became omnipresent. Riding the subway became an anxiety-provoking ritual fueled by a barrage of haunting messages: "Beware of suspicious packages. Bags are subject to random search by the police. If you see any suspicious activity on the platform or train notify a police officer, please remain alert and have a safe day." Machine gun-toting military officials patrolled the subway stations while police officers inspected straphangers' backpacks. Privacy was unanimously forfeited during the onset of the "War on Terror," and still nobody felt safe. In tandem, aggressive gentrification was rapidly taking place throughout the boroughs, displacing artists and native working class communities while simultaneously diminishing public space, independent businesses, and grassroots cultural centers. Luxury condos spread like wildfire in every borough, razing much of New York City's historic landscape. Infamous venues that had served as homes to alternative subcultures became extinct as sterile, homogeneous establishments took their place.

Parades, Parties, and Protests

The alternative venues that remained became the life-blood for many New Yorkers who were driven to garner strength from their community and express turbulent emotions through the arts.

Two weeks before the one-year anniversary of 9/11, event organizer Missy Galore and venue owner Lenny Charles acknowledged that nobody in the local artist community had planned a memorial event. They quickly decided that the void needed to be filled, and Charles offered up the use of his venue "Walker Stage." In a matter of days the duo orchestrated "U Can't Fight Peace," a free multimedia tribute event that was made possible by individuals who donated their time and energy to cultivate an inspirational night of art, unity and remembrance. U Can't Fight Peace provided an uplifting creative platform for New Yorkers to bear witness to the tragedy of 9/11. Throughout the night, Walker Stage overflowed with visual art, videos, photography and memorial performances, including a surprise set by underground legends Ari Up and Nina Hagen. Witness art attracts public recognition to situations of great social importance that one cannot change, but for moral or emotional reasons must acknowledge. In the words of author Jan Cohen-Cruz: "Bearing witness uses heightened means to direct attention onto actions of social magnitude ... from a perspective that would otherwise be missing ... A person who bears witness to an injustice takes responsibility for that awareness" (Cohen-Cruz, 1998: 65).

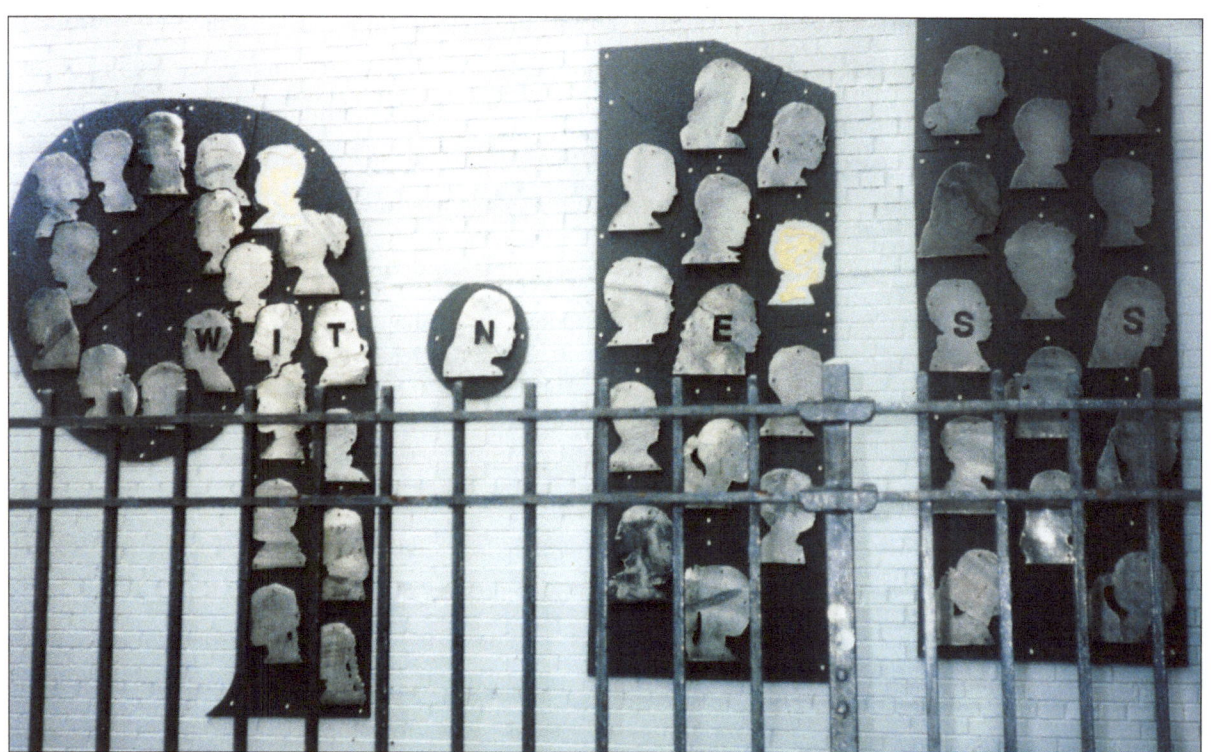

9/11 Witness installation at P.S. 20 in New York City, 2004

At U Can't Fight Peace, performance artist Amy Shapiro dramatized her experience of being on Wall Street the morning of the World Trade Center attack. She entered the room with her face concealed by a gas mask, then brazenly ripped off her clothes and wrapped herself in an American flag. Thick clouds of flour were catapulted into the air, simulating the ashes pouring from the iconic burning buildings. Amy's voice boomed over the audience with increasing urgency, as she recounted her harrowing experience of escaping downtown Manhattan that fateful day. During the finale of the performance, she withdrew a knife and plunged it into a big red apple. As the apple split in half, artificial blood cascaded down in an alarming conclusion that paid tribute to the city's broken heart.

One of the most striking Witness installations was designed by multimedia artist Judy Sky, who described it to me as a recreation of her arrival home to Manhattan from the 2001 Burning Man festival, just hours before the 9/11 terrorist attack. "My installation correlates my experiences of being at Burning Man and then returning to New York City on September 11th. Dust permeated everything at Burning Man, and the entire vicinity of the World Trade Center. The pile of dust covered shoes at the base of the installation, were inspired by a tragic photograph I had seen of shoes people ran out of in panic, scattered around Ground Zero. Also at Burning Man, a ubiquitous experience is for everyone's shoes to get totally covered with playa dust. The tree in the installation represents the tree of life, as well as the trees at the World Trade Center that were coated with dust and debris. The water bottles lit up with lights, were symbolic of the need for water in crisis situations."

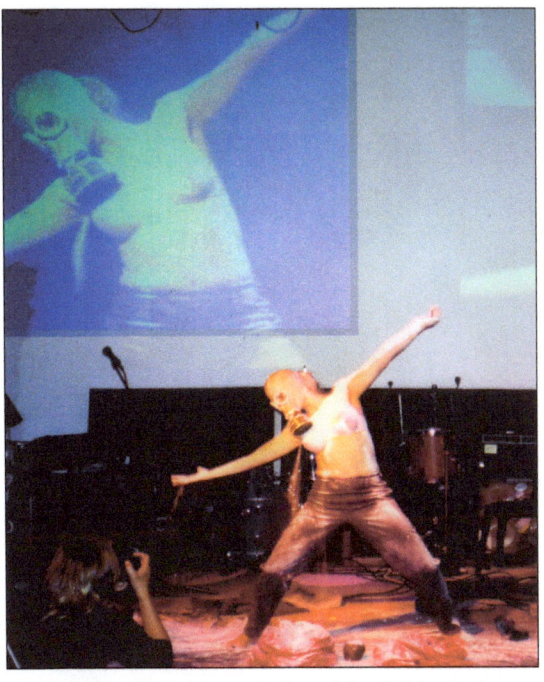

Amy Shapiro's interpretation of the 9/11 attacks at U Can't Fight Peace, September 11, 2002

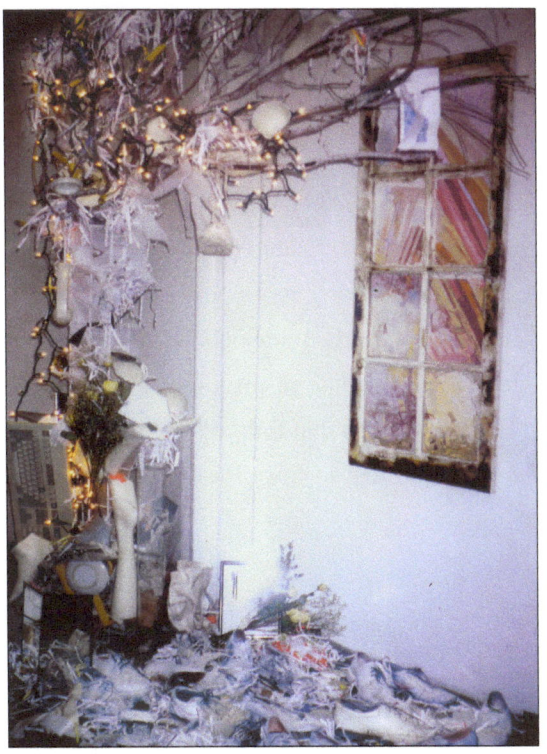

Ground Zero art installation by Judy Sky, 2002

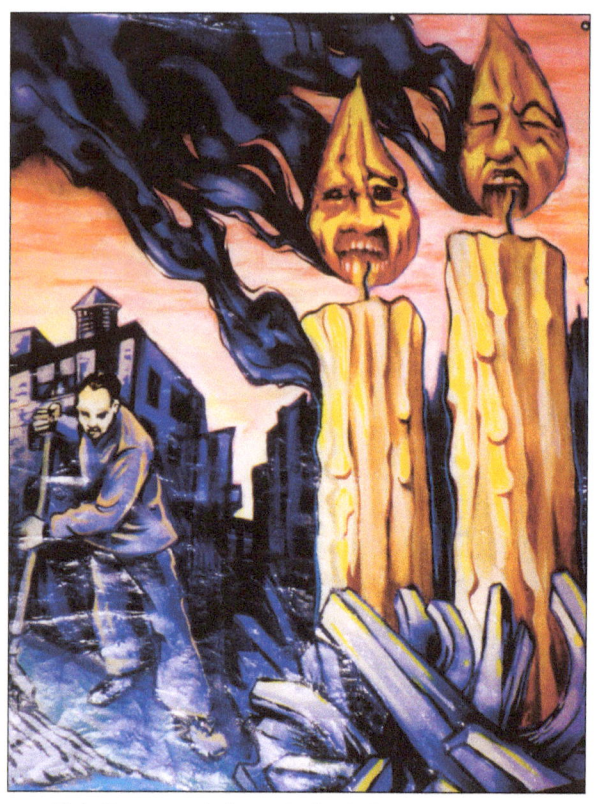

Twin Towers painting at U Can't Fight Peace, 2002

> ❝ **BEARING WITNESS USES HEIGHTENED MEANS TO DIRECT ATTENTION ONTO ACTIONS OF SOCIAL MAGNITUDE ... FROM A PERSPECTIVE THAT WOULD OTHERWISE BE MISSING ... A PERSON WHO BEARS WITNESS TO AN INJUSTICE TAKES RESPONSIBILITY FOR THAT AWARENESS ...** ❞

U Can't Fight Peace was one of many events over the following decade to provide a cathartic platform for bearing witness to the September 11th terrorist attacks. A variety of venues including galleries, libraries, and schools opened their doors to showcase 9/11 memorial art and to host tribute events. This vulnerable time heightened the need for community spaces that provided a service beyond the realm of commerce: places where people could go to foster kinship and support while cultivating vital sanctuary and renewal. In the wake of 9/11, Witness art served as an invaluable tool to process painful emotions that arose during a time of profound transition and turmoil. The tragic events that occurred on September 11th and the wars that followed marked a turning point in American history that would transform cultural identity, national security, foreign policy and international relations for many years to come.

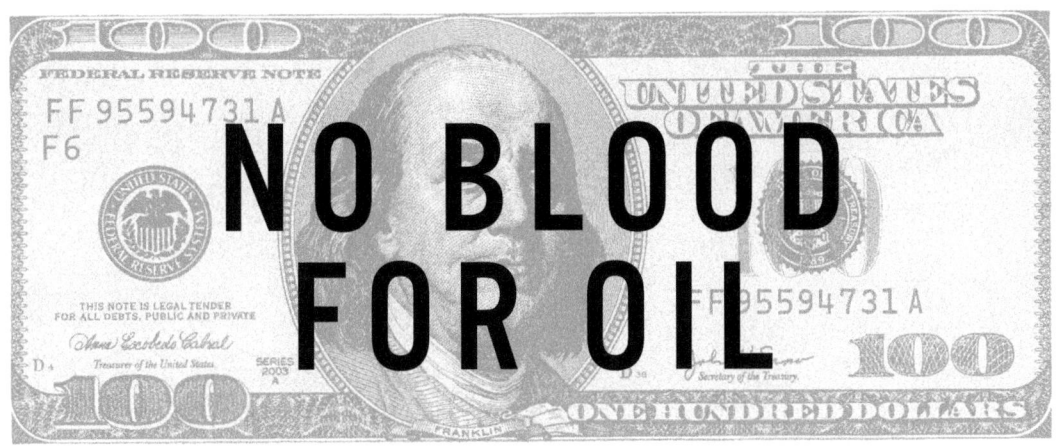

NO BLOOD FOR OIL

THE BUSH ADMINISTRATION & THE IRAQ WAR

In the aftermath of the terrorist attacks on September 11th, 2001, the Bush administration declared preemptive war on any organization or individual deemed a threat to national security. The origin of the U.S. policy on preemptive war was first drafted in 1992 in the "Defense Planning Guidance" report compiled by former Under Secretary of Defense Paul Wolfowitz (PBS, 2003). This doctrine was expanded in 1997 following the formation of the Project for a New American Century (PNAC), an organization whose prominent members included Wolfowitz, Donald Rumsfeld, Jeb Bush, and Dick Cheney. Three years later, in September 2000, the PNAC issued a report titled "Rebuilding America's Defenses," which underlined its core belief that "America should seek to preserve and extend its position of global leadership by maintaining the preeminence of U.S. military forces (Donnelly, 2000)." The Project for the New American Century sought to build a Pax Americana (Latin for "American Peace") that specifically focused on dominating the Middle East by targeting Iraq's oil to fund wars in Afghanistan, Iran, Syria, Korea and Lebanon. Many of the PNAC's founding members rose to prominent positions of power in the Bush administration and proceeded to shape U.S. foreign policy with the tenets of increased military spending and preemptive war.

On March 20th, 2003, the United States launched an unlawful war against the sovereign state of Iraq in violation of the Nuremberg Charter and the United Nations Security Council (BBC News, 2004). The Iraq occupation had the lowest poll approval of all modern U.S. wars[1], and consequently inspired the largest protest movement in history. Many of the Bush administration's justifications for going to war were not based on substantiated evidence. Unfounded speculations included Iraq's

---

1 *According to an Associated Press/Ipsos poll taken in January 2007, more than 70 percent of Americans were against the Iraq war (MSNBC, 2007).*

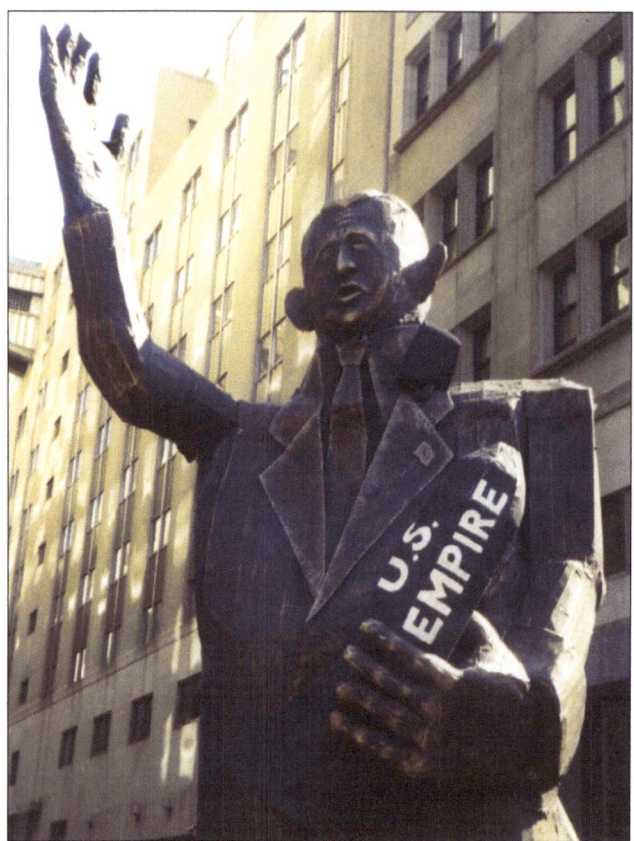

"The World Still Says 'No' to War" protest
New York City, 2004

" WE CANNOT ARREST [BUSH AND BLAIR], WE CANNOT DETAIN THEM, AND WE CANNOT HANG THEM THE WAY THEY HANGED SADDAM HUSSEIN... IN HISTORY BOOKS THEY SHOULD BE WRITTEN DOWN AS WAR CRIMINALS AND THIS IS THE KIND OF PUNISHMENT WE CAN MAKE TO THEM "

involvement with the September 11th terrorist attacks and Saddam Hussein's alleged possession of weapons of mass destruction. In August 2002, former Vice President Dick Cheney asserted: "There is no doubt that Saddam Hussein possesses weapons of mass destruction… He is amassing them to use against our friends, our allies, and against us" (Miller, 2006: 22). This bold proclamation on behalf of the former Vice President was proven false by an array of experts in the international community.[2] Amidst the U.S. rush to battle, United Nations weapons inspectors were forced to halt their investigation and ordered to abruptly exit Iraq. Far from saving it as a last resort, the U.S. government opted to initiate war and all the misery it entails as a preemptive first choice.

When Iraq's weapons of mass destruction failed to materialize, the justification of the subsequent initiative was to achieve "Iraqi liberation" from their merciless dictator, Saddam Hussein. Under the guise of bringing "freedom and democracy" to the Iraqi people, the U.S. unleashed a Pandora's box of violence and chaos.

---

2 *"In December 2002, Iraq produced a nearly 12,000 page report to account for its weapons program showing that all weapons stock piles had been destroyed… In February 2003 Hands Blix 2nd report had inspected thousands of sites, and turned up no evidence of a weapons program… In January 2004, David Kay the Chief American weapons inspector in Iraq tells Senate that no weapons of mass destruction have been found, and that pre-war intelligence was wrong" (Miller, 2006: 23).*

The death toll mounted daily: by January 2012, more than 100,000 Iraqi civilians had been killed since the onset of the U.S.-led occupation (Iraq Body Count, 2012). Over 4,000 U.S. troops died serving in Iraq, while thousands more returned home physically maimed and suffering from debilitiating posttraumatic stress-related illnesses.

In February 2007, the U.S. House of Representatives held a conference to debate the Bush administration's proposed "troop surge" in Iraq. The debate revealed that many members of Congress felt deceived by the Bush administration – especially

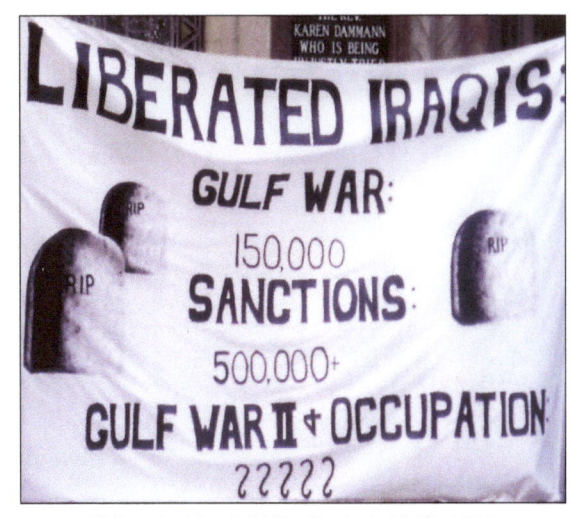

"Liberated Iraqis" War Protest, NYC, 2004

those who had voted in favor of the war – because they were told in no uncertain terms that Iraq posed an immediate terrorist threat to America. No weapons of mass destruction or direct links to the terrorist organizations Al Qaeda or the Taliban were ever found. Members of the House had also been told that oil revenue from Iraq would help pay for the war. Paradoxically, the ongoing occupation caused the U.S. to accumulate more than a trillion dollars of national debt.[3] The debate in the House of Representatives culminated with the majority voting against further funding of the Iraq war, with 246 Representatives standing against the troop increase and 182 choosing to "hold the course" (Open Congress, 2007). This debate was not a binding resolution. Despite earning the disapproval of the majority of U.S. citizens and the House of Representatives, the Bush administration intensified the occupation. Full withdrawal of U.S. troops from Iraq was scheduled in the Status of Forces Agreement for January 1st, 2012 (Al Jazeera, 2008).

The Bush administration had deeply entrenched financial interests in perpetuating the Iraq war, with a checkered history tied to the oil and weapons industry and surreptitious business relationships with "Axis of Evil" dictator Saddam Hussein and members of the notorious bin Laden family. In 1977, George W. Bush launched his own oil drilling company, Arbusto Energy, with financial backing from bin Laden family heir Salem bin Laden via his representative James R. Bathe (Madsen, 2002). During George W. Bush's first term as

---

3 *Representative Emanuel from Illinois: "For the past 5 years we have accepted the President's assurances on Iraq, only to learn that the facts on the ground belied his aggressive assertions and rosy rhetoric. We accepted his assurances about the presence of weapons of mass destruction and Saddam's links to al Qaeda. We authorized a war on that basis, only to learn that much of what we were told simply wasn't true." Representative Gutierrez of Illinois: "We were told that future oil revenues would more than cover the cost of the reconstruction. They could not have been more wrong. The cost of the war continues to grow at an outrageous rate. To date, we have spent approximately $379 billion on this war, with estimates from some experts saying that the total long-term cost could exceed $1 trillion dollars" (Truemajority.org, 2007).*

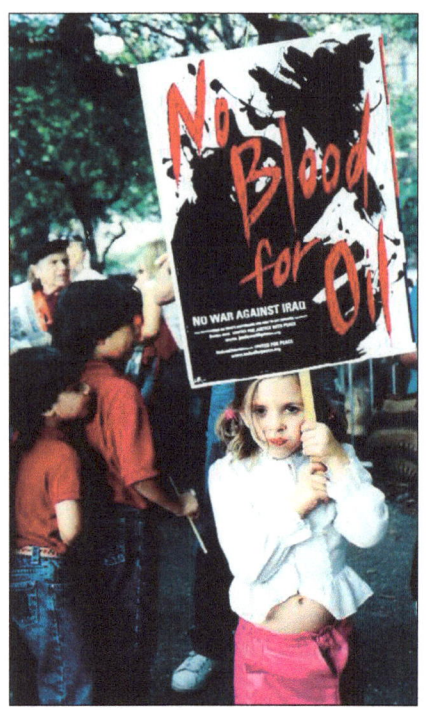

Felix Chrome, protests the Iraq War, NYC, 2003

president, his father George H. Bush was appointed senior advisor to the private investment firm The Carlyle Group. The Saudi bin Laden Group, a holding company for the bin Laden family assets, had invested in Carlyle for years, specifically in the war-driven "Partner 2 Fund." The Partner 2 Fund included United Defense and other weapons manufacturers that produced combat vehicles and weapons delivery systems. This business arrangement was auspiciously severed in October 2001 (Golden, 2001).

In 1983, the Bush's Defense Secretary Donald Rumsfeld attempted to negotiate a contract with Saddam Hussein on behalf of the Bechtel Corporation (Herbert, 2003). Hussein failed to approve the $2 billion oil pipeline proposed by the United States. In April 2003, The Bechtel Corporation won the second largest contract worth $680 million to help rebuild post-war Iraq (Miller, 2006: xiv). Condoleezza Rice, National Security Advisor of the Bush Administration, was the director of the Chevron Oil Company from 1991 to January 2001. Former Vice President Dick Cheney was the Chairman and Chief Executive of Dallas-based Halliburton Corporation, the world's largest oil field service company, from 1995 to 2000. Halliburton holds multi-billion dollar contracts with oil corporations such as Chevron, and had done $73 million dollars in business between 1997-2000 with Saddam Hussein's Iraq (Baum, 2003). With egregious war profiteering reaching unprecedented new levels, Halliburton Corporation received the largest contracts to rebuild post-war Iraq. In November 2002, the Pentagon awarded Halliburton the first no-bid contracts for post-war repairs of Iraq's oil industry – nearly five months before the war began. In March 2003, the U.S. Army Corps of Engineers granted Halliburton a contract worth more than a billion dollars to rehabilitate Iraq's oil industry. Halliburton got caught overcharging the U.S. Army Corps by more than $200 million for its services.[4] No criminal charges were ever filed against Halliburton executives.

For eight years, the Bush administration fostered the erosion of several central tenets of the U.S. Constitution, including the right to privacy, security against unlawful search and seizure, freedom of assembly,

---

4 *"The largest single recipient of Iraqi funds was Halliburton, the oil services firm once led by U.S. Vice Pres. Dick Cheney, which received $1.6 billion in Iraqi oil proceeds under a contract to import fuel and repair oil fields. According to DCAA auditors, Halliburton's overcharges under this contract are more than $218 million" (Fisher, 2005).*

habeus corpus and the right to due process.[5] As a result, many Americans were left feeling powerless to protest or even vote. All the while, domestic surveillance was being ramped up with the passage of invasive laws such as the PATRIOT Act, which legalized spying on U.S. citizens. The PATRIOT Act sanctioned the surveillance of Americans' phone calls, emails, and financial records, as well as taking people into custody without a court order (Savage, 2011). As author Tom Robbins poignantly noted: "When freedom is outlawed, only the outlaws will be free" (Robbins, 1980).

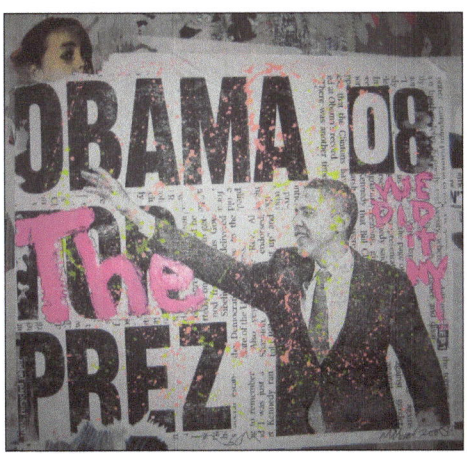

Obama street art, New York City, 2008

During the 2008 presidential election, the Barack Obama campaign mobilized millions of alienated Americans to vote by encouraging involvement in a participatory democracy. The historic election of the first African-American president imparted a brief sense of hope and elation for many citizens in a largely despairing and apathetic nation. This was quickly overshadowed by the sober reality of the extensive damage left in the aftermath of the Bush administration, and the institution of ongoing legislation that infringes upon American's civil liberties and borders on martial law (Kuhner, 2012).

In the wake of a myriad of atrocities, citizens all over the world petitioned for the trial of George W. Bush, Dick Cheney and other top Bush administration officials for crimes and misdemeanors, including illegal wiretapping, torturing prisoners, and the unjust occupation of Iraq. In a symbolic trial on November 22, 2011, the Kuala Lumpur War Crimes Commission in Malaysia reached a unanimous verdict that found George W. Bush and his ally former British Prime Minister Tony Blair guilty of crimes against peace, crimes against humanity, and genocide as a result of their roles in spearheading the Iraq War (Falk, 2011). The tribunal acknowledged that its verdict was not enforceable by law, yet committed to reporting the findings of guilt of the two former heads of state to the International Criminal Court in the Hague, and entered the names of Bush and Blair in the Register of War Criminals maintained by the KLWCC. The former Malaysian head of state, Mahathir Mohamed declared: "We cannot arrest them, we cannot detain them, and we cannot hang them the way they hanged Saddam Hussein... In history books they should be written down as war criminals and this is the kind of punishment we can make to them" (Falk, 2011).

---

5 *Representative DeGette: "We defend our constitutional process when we demand that the President listen to the American people and end unilateral actions that undermine our nation's strength and place our troops in an untenable, lethal and unwinnable situation...I did not come here to watch our Constitution be rewritten by presidential arrogance and disregard...I did not come here to ignore the American people who want this war stopped now" (Truemajority.org).*

" CORPORATIONS HAVE BEEN ENTHRONED AND AN ERA OF CORRUPTION IN HIGH PLACES WILL FOLLOW, AND THE MONEY POWER OF THE COUNTRY WILL ENDEAVOR TO PROLONG ITS REIGN BY WORKING UPON THE PREJUDICES OF THE PEOPLE UNTIL WEALTH IS AGGREGATED IN A FEW HANDS ... AND THE REPUBLIC IS DESTROYED. "

– PRESIDENT ABRAHAM LINCOLN

NOV. 21, 1864
LETTER TO COL. WILLIAM F. ELKINS

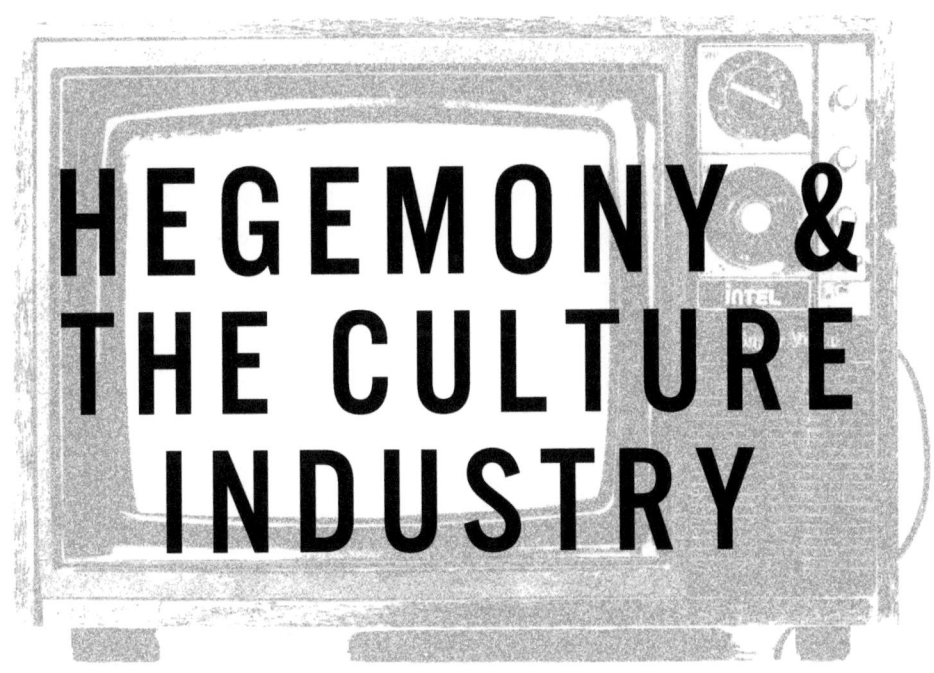

HEGEMONY & THE CULTURE INDUSTRY

The United States of America was born from a revolution against the British monarchy and corporations, culminating with the Declaration of Independence in 1776. As America redefined itself as a sovereign nation, restrictions were placed on how large and powerful corporations could become. Their right to contribute financially to electoral campaigns was revoked in order to curtail the influence of big business over politicians. However, the Civil War marked a turning point. While capitalizing on the instability of the country, war became a profitable venture for many U.S. corporations. They made huge profits from procurement contracts and took advantage of the disorder of the times to buy legislators. President Abraham Lincoln warned that the ethos of a democratic society would be destroyed if big business gained too much power: "Corporations have been enthroned... An era of corruption in high places will follow until wealth is aggregated in a few hands... and the republic is destroyed" (Lasn, 1999: 67). President Lincoln's advice went unheeded and American corporations continued to gain insurmountable influence.

Shortly after the Civil War, in a legal twist that many do not understand to this day, corporations obtained the ultimate benefits of American society by being declared "natural persons" under the U.S. Constitution – an outcome resulting from the 1886 U.S. Supreme Court case *Santa Clara County v. Southern Pacific Railroad* (Lasn, 1999:68). Corporate personhood eroded American democracy as big businesses gained protection under the Bill of Rights and acquired the ability to contribute financially to political campaigns. With exponentially more resources at their disposal than that of individual citizens, corporations then proceeded to manipulate politics, and absorb the majority of local media outlets and independent entrepreneurs, thus paving over the face of society with their logos.

The dictatorial impact corporate monopolies have on society was outlined in 1845 by Karl Marx and Fredrick Engel in *The Ruling Class and the Ruling Ideas*, which states: "The class that is the ruling material force of society is at the same time it's ruling intellectual force... so the ideas of those who lack the means of material production are subject to it" (Marx and Engels, 2001: 39). This ideology was the basis for Italian Marxist Antonio Gramsci's concept of "hegemony," which asserts the ruling class molds the intellectual framework of society so that their authority and principles appear "legitimate and natural."[6] Neo-Marxist theorists Theodor Adorno and Max Horkheimer of the Frankfurt School believed that the "culture industry," the system that produces mass culture, is the leading force in establishing hegemony in modern society (Adorno and Horkheimer, 1996:71). The upper echelon owns the means of production and therefore controls the flow of ideas by manufacturing mass culture including television, film, music, books, and newspapers. The products of the culture industry are predominantly used as tools for upholding ruling class ideologies and distracting the public with sensationalism. The Frankfurt School acknowledged that the culture industry had become the central fixture of modern society, and was being used as an agent of control, permeating every aspect of the social order.

The culture industry of the 21st century threatens democracy and freedom of expression by utilizing the process of "vertical integration," in which transnational corporations monopolize the majority of communication channels.[7] In June 2003, the Republican-controlled Federal Communications Commission (FCC) voted to increase the consolidation of mass media outlets by America's largest conglomerates from 35 to 45 percent, diminishing long-standing restrictions on the number of newspapers, television channels, and radio stations that one company could own (Labaton, 2003). The FCC's policies aid the mega-corporations in maximizing profits and conveying ideologies that serve their best interests by limiting

---

6 *Hegemony*: *Used to suggest a society in which, despite oppression and exploitation, there is a high degree of "consensus;" a society in which subordinate groups and classes appear to actively support and subscribe to values, ideals, objectives cultural and political meanings, which "incorporate" them into the prevailing structures of power (Storey, 2003:49).*

7 *Vertical Integration*: *The flow of information worldwide is controlled by an ever-shrinking number of transnational media corporations... Time Warner, Disney, Bertelsmann, Viacom, and Rupert Murdoch's News Corporation. The great power of these organizations lies in their vertical integration. They produce a film, and distribute it through their own theater chain, promote it through their own TV networks, play the soundtrack on their own radio stations and sell the merchandising spin offs at their own amusement parks (Lasn, 1999:26).*

"THE CLASS THAT IS THE RULING MATERIAL FORCE OF SOCIETY IS ... IT'S RULING INTELLECTUAL FORCE... SO THE IDEAS OF THOSE WHO LACK THE MEANS OF MATERIAL PRODUCTION ARE SUBJECT TO IT"

– KARL MARX & FREDRICK ENGEL 1845

the transmission of diverse information and perspectives. Visual content that has the potential to incite a cultural revolution is excluded from the mass media. When Americans turned on the television in 2003, they did not see footage of millions of people protesting the Iraq war on the streets of New York City, Los Angeles, San Francisco, and Washington D.C., nor did they see photos of American soldiers returning home in caskets or mutilated Iraqi children littering the streets of Baghdad. During the 1960s, the graphic images of the Vietnam War and the accompanying protest movements were broadcast on national television. These images helped mobilize a generation that would be defined by a flamboyant nation-wide youth rebellion.

Laws have been implemented to protect citizens from manipulation by the media, yet corporate monopolies over communication outlets make these regulations nearly impossible to enforce. According to Article 13 of the 1979 American Convention on Human Rights: "The right of expression may not be restricted by indirect methods or means, such as abuse of government or private controls over newsprint, radio broadcasting... or any other means of tending to impede the communication and circulation of ideas and opinions (ACHR, 1992)." Corporate dominion over venues and mainstream media outlets results in homogeneous ideologies being conveyed from so many different angles that they appear to be common sense, even if they make no sense at all.

The onset of industrialization in America resulted in a large-scale shift away from close-knit communities and family businesses to a zeitgeist of impersonal jobs, instant gratification consumerism, and loss of the kinship network. This rendered people more susceptible to buying into an ideology system created by the culture industry. The products of mass culture became compensation for lives that lacked meaning derived from cultural heritage, spirituality, or personalized labor. Under the guise of entertainment, mass culture provides a system of fleeting status symbols that encourages people to consume incessantly in order to keep up with an ever-changing status quo.

The culture industry exploits consumers' fantasies and insecurities by broadcasting glamorized images of beauty, pleasure, and status portrayed as attainable through purchase. Emaciated, digitally enhanced females and muscle-bound males are featured in advertisements to encourage people to buy more booze, buy more clothes, buy more cars, buy more cosmetics, and buy more electronics. This constant bombardment subliminally fuels feelings of inadequacy. Consumers are left with a hopeless sense of not having enough and a hunger for countless commodities designed with built-in obsolescence. The coercive nature of mass culture indoctrinates people to think they need more, forcing them to work longer and harder to obtain more (or consequently live far beyond their means and accrue massive amounts of debt). As a result, many people have less free time to be politically active, cultivate community, spend quality time with friends and family, make art, or think for themselves.[8] Concurrently, the culture industry's stronghold is reinforced, while adults work increasingly long hours to make ends meet, and entire generations of children are being raised by television, video games, and online social networks.

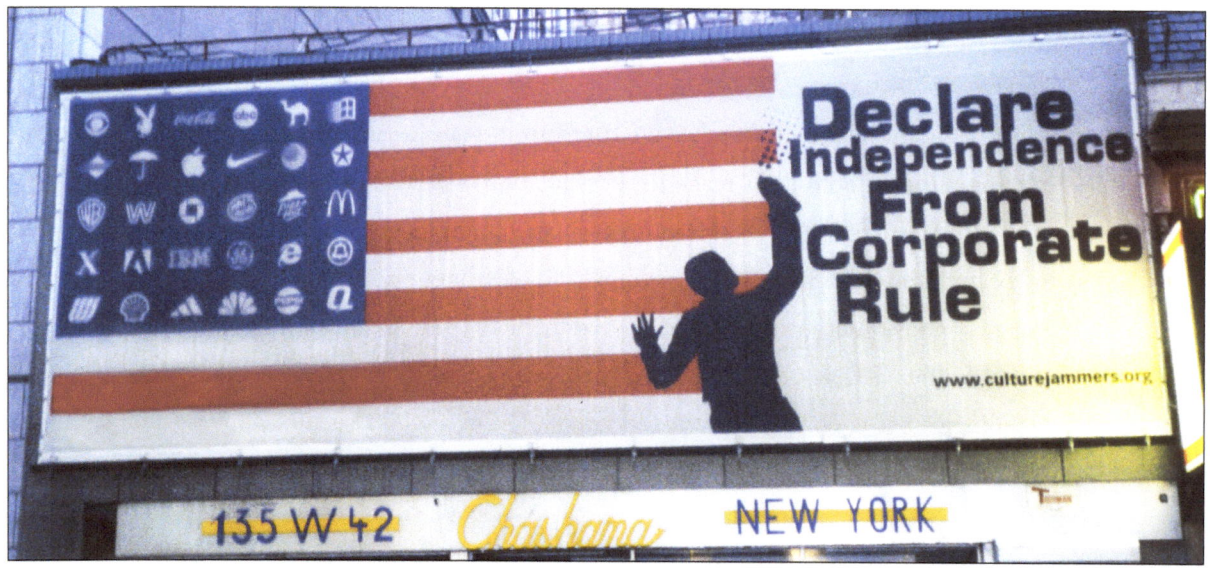

Culture Jam billboard at Chashama Theater on 42nd Street, New York City, 2002

---

8 *"The cultural commodities produced by the culture industry make up a system… in which deceived masses are caught in a 'circle of manipulation and retroactive need in which the unity of the system grows even stronger.' The culture industry has… to arrest and imprison our cultural and political imaginations, thus making it increasingly impossible to think outside the prevailing structures of power" (Kellner, Durham, 2001: 29).*

Another fundamental function of the 21ˢᵗ century culture industry is to facilitate the absorption of resistance culture. Corporations hire savvy trend scouts to scour the city streets in search of individuals with cutting-edge styles in order to co-opt them into flashy advertising campaigns and mainstream clothing lines. Electronic music that was once the subversive anthem of the underground rave scene is now used in television commercials to sell sports cars. The rebellious stance of alternative fashion staples, such as fishnets, leather, latex, safety pins, and spikes, is rendered obsolete once reproduced and sold to the masses at local shopping malls. In the 1960s, participants of the counterculture wore long hair, beads, and bell-bottoms. These visual emblems became synonymous with revolution and opposition to the Vietnam War. The resistance culture of the 21ˢᵗ century is much harder to identify: it is diverse and chameleonic, casting off previous generation's uniforms of resistance in order to survive.

Monopolies over mainstream media channels deny a large portion of the population the ability to contribute in molding society. With mounting corporate influence, the majority of culture generated is profit-driven, and no longer the by-product of what people create as an expression of their history, or the inspiration that moves their soul. Rich cultural heritages and ecosystems around the world are being annihilated by the encroachment of a vacuous corporate monoculture.[9] If we want to live according to the tenets of freedom and democracy, individuals must make conscious choices to reclaim their mental environments by not rampantly consuming the culture industry's programs and products. Corporations must be stripped of their rights as natural citizens and stringent laws must be enforced that disarm them from monopolizing mass-communication outlets and funding political campaigns, so that mass media and the U.S. government can truly represent and serve the people of the nation.

---

9 *"When a handful of mega-corporations control; not only the daily newspapers and TV airwaves but the magazines, book publishing, motion picture, home video and music industry as well, information and cultural diversity plummet. In all systems, homogenization is poison. Lack of diversity... the loss of a language, tradition, or heritage... is as big of a loss to future genera-tions" (Lasn, 1999: 25).*

" WE HAVE TO FIND OUR OWN FORMS OF GESTURE AND COMMUNICATION. YOU CAN NEVER DEPEND ON THE MASS MEDIA TO REFLECT US OR OUR NEEDS OR STATE OF MIND. "

– DAVID WOJNAROWICZ

POSTCARDS FROM AMERICA: X-RAYS FROM HELL
(1989)

PUBLIC SPACE, AGITPROP & RADICAL STREET THEATER

As a declaration of opposition to the erosion of civil liberties, economic inequality, corporate dominion, and on-going wars, savvy activists penetrate the barriers of established social protocol by infiltrating public by-ways and special events with cunning parodies of current tribulations. On the streets of New York, oil covered sirens and suit-clad loan sharks strut side-by-side down Surf Avenue at the annual Coney Island Mermaid Day Parade. George W. Bush made several "guest appearances" at the Greenwich Village Halloween Parade dressed as a cowboy, a weasel, a toilet bowl, and Adolf Hitler. Opulently dressed billionaires attended anti-war demonstrations brandishing signs that said: "Fuck the Poor." Agitprop radical street theater is a visual art and performance-based protest medium that is designed to publicly expose corruption and injustice. Agitprop is derived from the words "agitation" and "propaganda," and describes art forms with an explicitly political message. Armed with art and ideology, vigilant activists take to the streets to combat white-collar abuses of power. In the fight for social justice and community sovereignty, the street is a stage for the showdown.

The constitutional liberties of free expression and assembly have a symbiotic relationship with public space; one cannot survive without the other. If freedom of expression is going to materialize beyond the theoretical, it needs a place in which to exist. Non-commercial public space is rapidly dwindling as it is usurped by private enterprises for the sake of generating profits and exerting social control. In the face of sweeping gentrification, community gardens are carved up and sold off to luxury housing developers.

Parades, Parties, and Protests

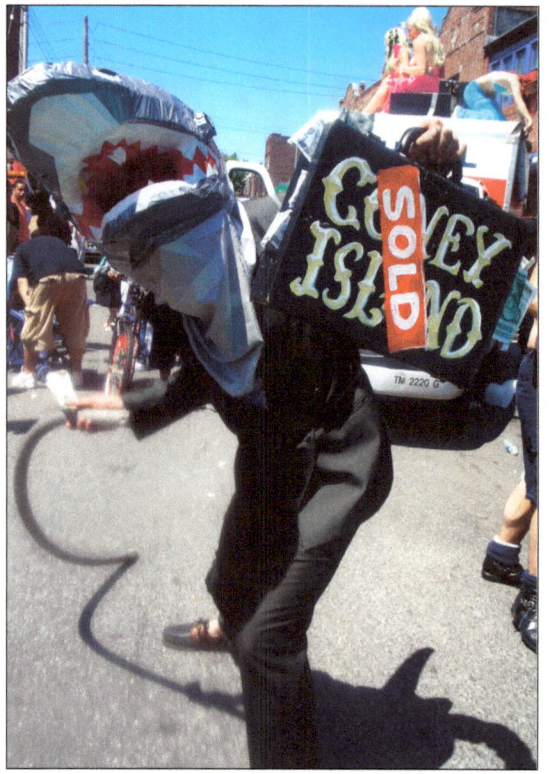

"Money Shark" corporate development protest at the Coney Island Mermaid Parade, 2007

Public parks shrink in size as regulations for their use increase. Permits for outdoor community gatherings and activist demonstrations become increasingly hard to obtain. Vehicles, advertising, and commerce monopolize the streets. Chain stores systematically eliminate independently owned businesses. Socialization options are largely contingent on consumption in restaurants, bars and shopping malls. A life prescribed – but only for those who can afford it. The privatization of public space diminishes quality of life for countless individuals whose ability to congregate is increasingly marginalized.

As media monopolies exponentially expand and our public spaces are sold off to the highest bidder, Agitprop radical street theater creates a public forum for expression of alternative perspectives that is both free and priceless. Radical street theater challenges the status quo by combining activism with visual art and performances that are spontaneously executed in conventional public spaces and cultural events. Amidst vibrant public celebrations, iconic political representations employ parody to convey outrageous socio-political conditions, alongside whimsical characters and imagery designed to invoke

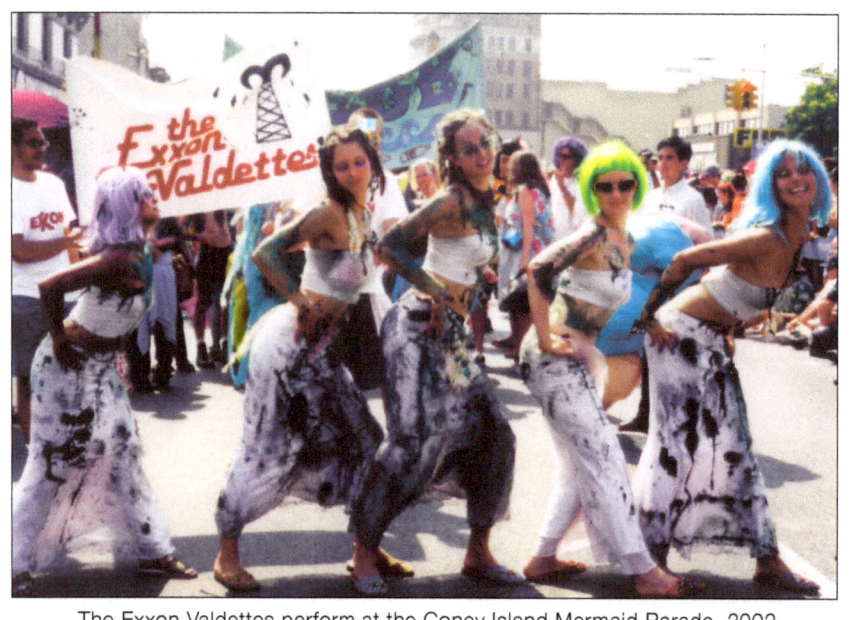

The Exxon Valdettes perform at the Coney Island Mermaid Parade, 2002

a semblance of an ideal world. The art-based Agitprop protest style is the framework for radical street theater, where performance, puppetry, costuming, and signage are incorporated to raise awareness about pressing social concerns while occupying public by-ways in order to provide outreach to a diverse audience.

One of the most innovative organizations to orchestrate radical Agitprop street protests is Bread and Puppet Theater, whose larger-than-life political puppet street performances influenced generations of creative dissent movements. Bread and Puppet is one of the oldest non-profit theatrical companies in the U.S., founded by Peter Shumann in 1962 on New York City's Lower East Side.[10] The original puppet-based protests emerged as a public outcry against the Vietnam War. Bread and Puppet staged block-long processions depicting the arrogance of warmongers and the despair of their victims. Bread and

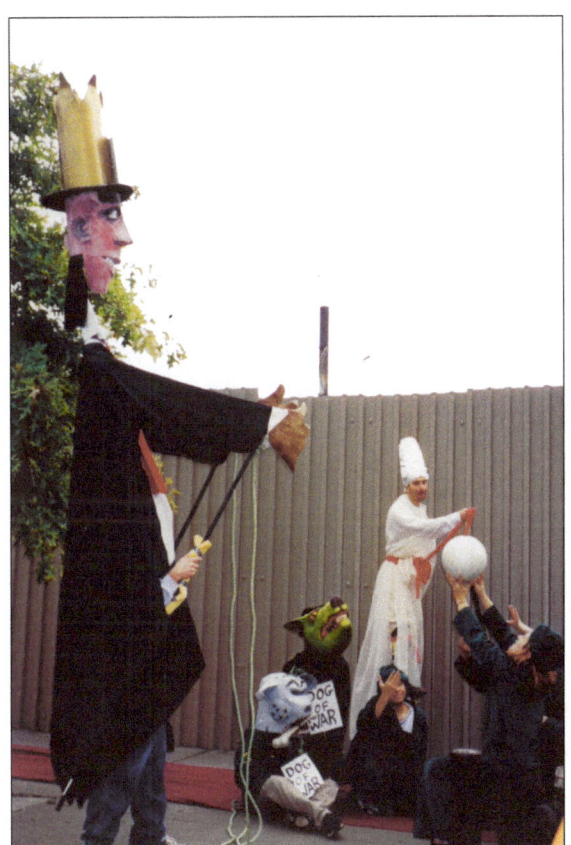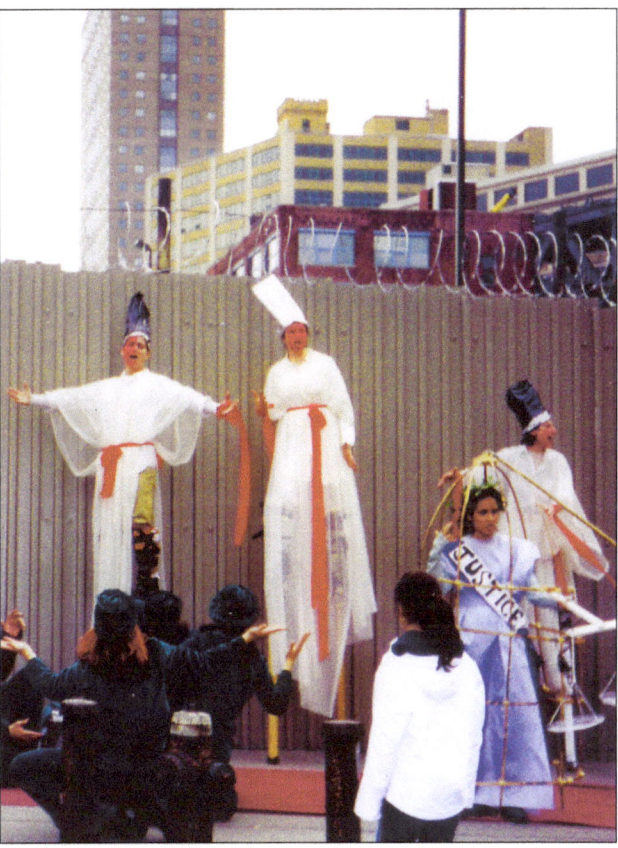

Bread and Puppet Theater war protest at the DUMBO Arts Festival in Brooklyn, 2002

10   *Shumann's innovation of the puppet theater as modern political art form is a live interruption of everyday public life, as a successful means of speaking out in a political fashion in ways, which mass-communicated media cannot or will not do. The parade can reach large numbers of people directly, outside the bounds of mass media. To avoid solely "preaching to the converted" it publicly asserts a dissenting voice, it bears witness to the voices silenced by the mass media (Cohen-Cruz and Bell, 1998: 275).*

PARADES, PARTIES, AND PROTESTS

Puppet Theater marched into the 21st century using Agitprop street performance to declare opposition to the Iraq war. In October 2002 on the streets of DUMBO, Brooklyn, Bread and Puppet dramatized the pending atrocities with a 12-foot tall puppet of George W. Bush in full imperial attire and a dozen actors portraying "Justice" and the "Dogs of War."

Agitprop is a visually expressive style of activism that is traditionally associated with war protests, and is also used to raise awareness about a variety of other underpublicized political issues. In July 2002, a grassroots environmental group called "Recycle This" staged a protest outside of City Hall Park when Mayor Bloomberg bypassed New York State law and eliminated New York City's recycling program. Dozens of bottle-clad recycling enthusiasts erected a makeshift flower garden on the City Hall lawn crafted entirely from used bottles and cans in an effort to draw attention to the wasteful quandary at hand. Recycle This activists also distributed flyers listing facts about the essential functions of recycling and waste reduction in preserving planet Earth. The flyers provided the phone numbers for the Mayor and Attorney General to encourage constituents to actively petition their representatives and demand that the recycling program be reinstated.

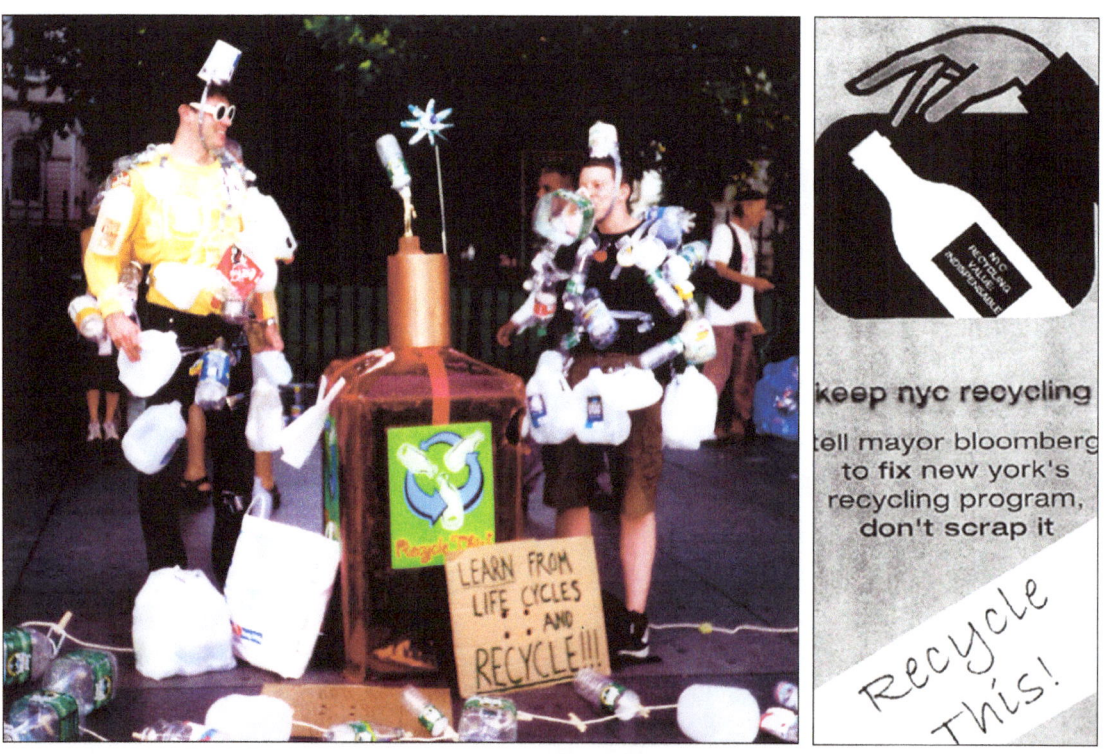

"Recycle This" demonstration outside of City Hall in response to
Mayor Bloomberg cutting New York City's recycling program, 2002

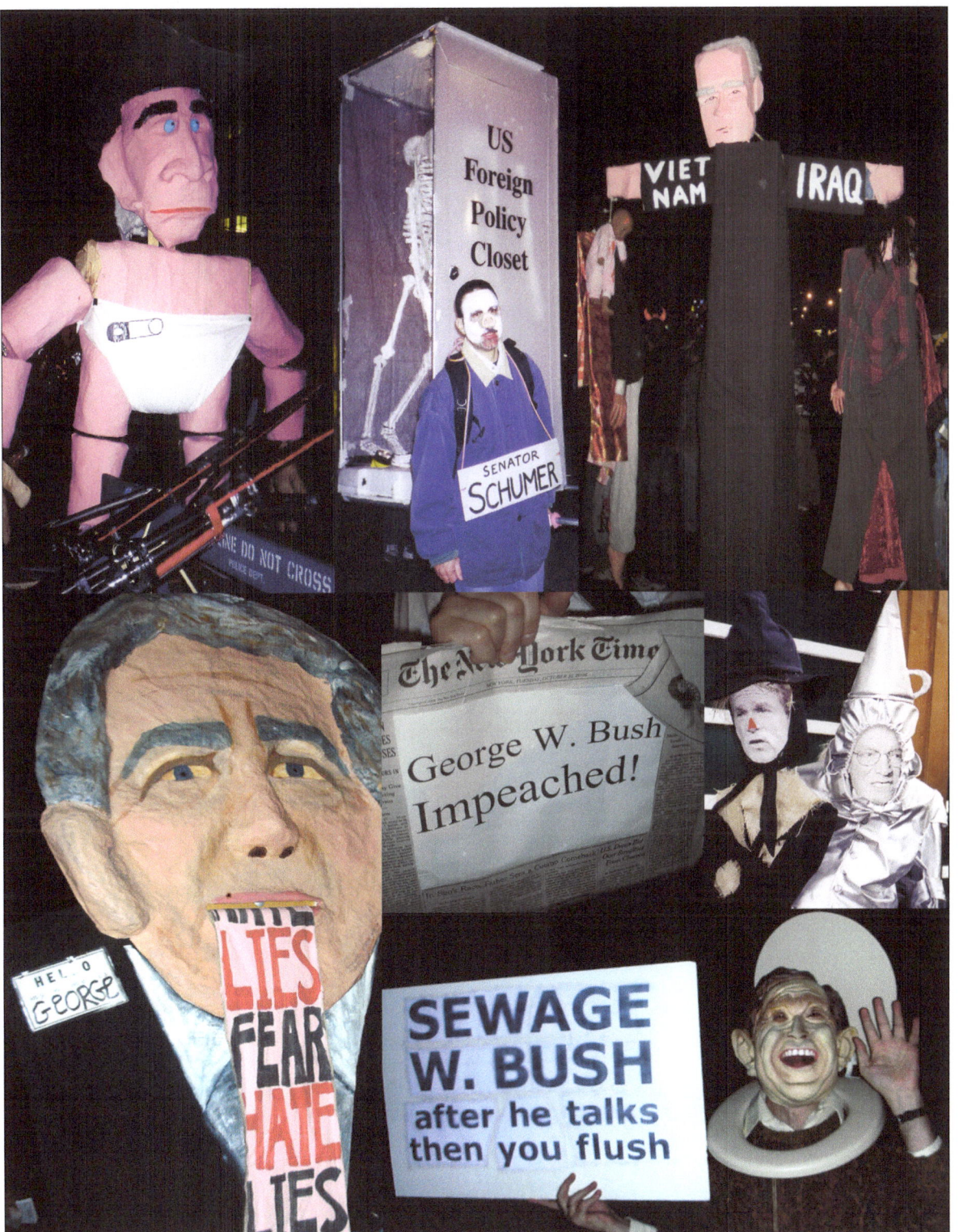

George W. Bush and friends at the Greenwich Village Halloween Parade, 2002-2008

Parades, Parties, and Protests

Parades are a frequent destination for Agitprop demonstrations, because these festive spectacles are one of the few remaining public platforms for social commentary. Amidst a sea of marching bands, Technicolor techno floats, drag queens and ghouls galore, the New York City Greenwich Village Halloween parade provided a public forum for expressing dissatisfaction with the Bush administration and U.S. foreign policy. During his near-decade long regime, the annual parade frequently featured costumes and sculptural floats of George W. Bush portrayed as a murderer, a warmonger and a liar, including "Sewage W. Bush," a radical street performer who sported a toilet seat on his head and a sign saying; "After He Talks, You Flush." In 2008, the notorious "Joe the Plumber" (an "average Joe" who was catapulted into a brief moment of celebrity as an iconic representative of the working class American during the 2008 presidential elections) made a special appearance at the Halloween Parade to help clean up after the boastful Republican presidential candidate John McCain's 15-foot-tall effigy which toured the parade with Vietnam and Iraq casualties of war in tow.

The social and environmental devastation inflicted on society as a result of white collar crimes committed by corporations and the government is largely downplayed or outright ignored by the mainstream media and is rarely punished by law.[11] In contrast, activists are often treated like terrorists and are depicted in the mass media with a slew of negative connotations. The mass media's focus on negative sensationalism often bypasses the true content and intentions of demonstrations, and fails to educate the public on why protests are taking place.[12] The culture industry does not represent the intelligence and ingenuity of activists because it does not serve the interests of the ruling class. This is why, according to the late visionary artist David Wojnarowicz: "We have to find our own forms of gesture and communication. You can never depend on the mass media to reflect us or our needs or state of mind" (Sheppard, 2002). In a time marked by burgeoning white-collar crime, protest is patriotic. Our liberties – and those of future generations – depend on it.

---

11 *Project Censored, the US media watchdog group, has released their annual report examining the shortcomings of reporting in 2012. Amongst the key topics: the rising police state and erosion of civil liberties, climate change and the destruction of oceans, and the rising disparity between the one percent and the 99 percent. Project Censored argues that the lack of proper reporting on issues like these by the corporate media is leading to an erosion of democracy (Al Jazeera, 2012).*

12 *We were occupying the city and dancing in its streets... We were making history. But when I left the demonstration and turned on the local news, I heard talks of rioters and chaos, not singing and dancing... I heard talk of a city driven to the brink of collapse by "angry protesters" and not an unjust system of exploitation creatively and beautifully stopped in its tracks (McCarty, 2003: 351).*

THE WORLD SAYS 'NO' TO WAR 2003

Demonstrations against the wars in Afghanistan and Iraq began in New York City just days after the September 11th attacks. While televisions across the country bombarded American households with 9/11 footage and a pro-war message, thousands of New Yorkers gathered in focal points around the city to publicly raise the flag for peace. One of the first organized demonstrations took place at Times Square, where hundreds of people congregated and stood silently, dressed in black, wearing dust masks, holding up stark, identical signs that read "Our Grief Is Not a Cry for War." On October 6th, 2002, more than 20,000 people converged in Central Park to pledge resistance and boldly declare "Not in Our Name" to the war in Afghanistan and the looming invasion of Iraq. The *Not In Our Name* demonstration was one of 30 that occurred over that weekend throughout the nation.

On January 11th, 2003, I attended Los Angeles' largest preemptive war protest on record. An estimated 15,000 people marched in a mile-long procession through the streets of downtown L.A. Many protesters donned elaborate costumes, colorful signs and large-scale puppets. The pulse of Korean drummers and Native American dancers enlivened the streets. Throngs of exuberant people sang, chanted and clapped for peace. The march culminated with a rally at the Federal Building, where numerous celebrities and activists took to the stage to publicly denounce the imminent acts of aggression against Iraq. The vibrant, multi-cultural Los Angeles demonstration made a bold proclamation: the citizens of the world stand for peace.

On February 15th, 2003, the *World Says 'No' to War* demonstration marked the largest day of protest in human history. More than ten million people in over 600 cities around the globe marched in solidarity

33

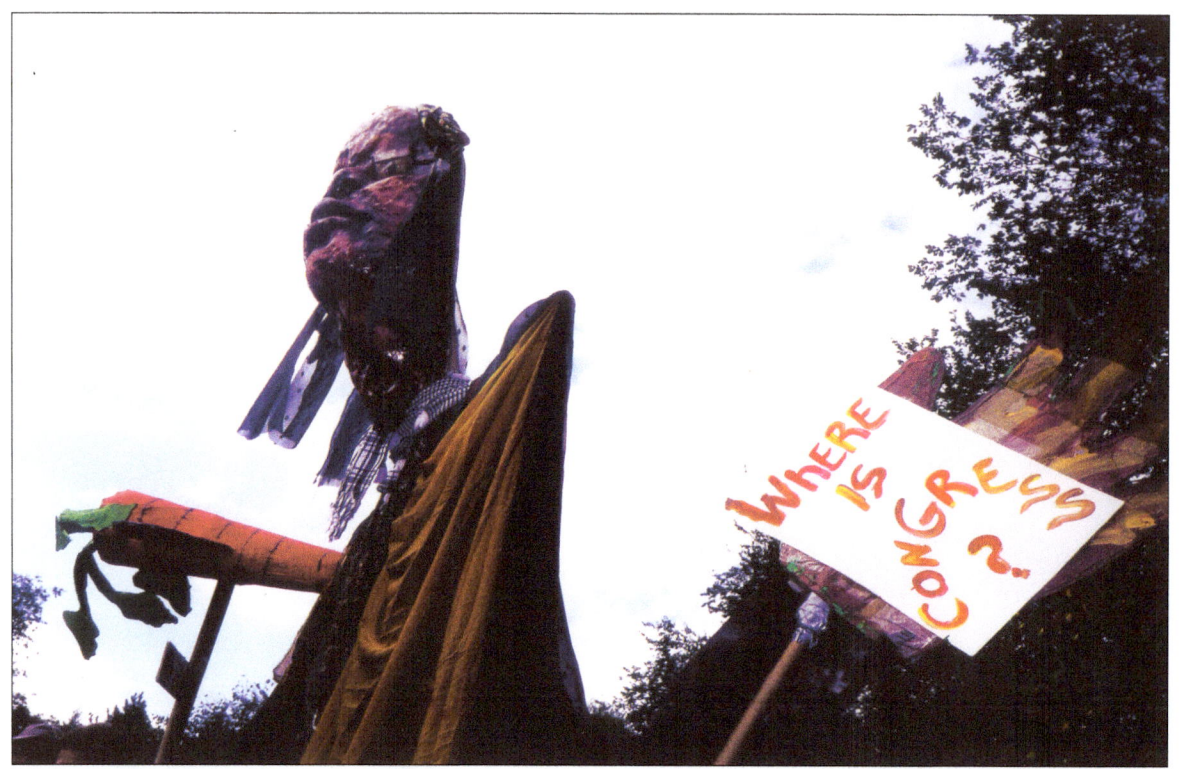

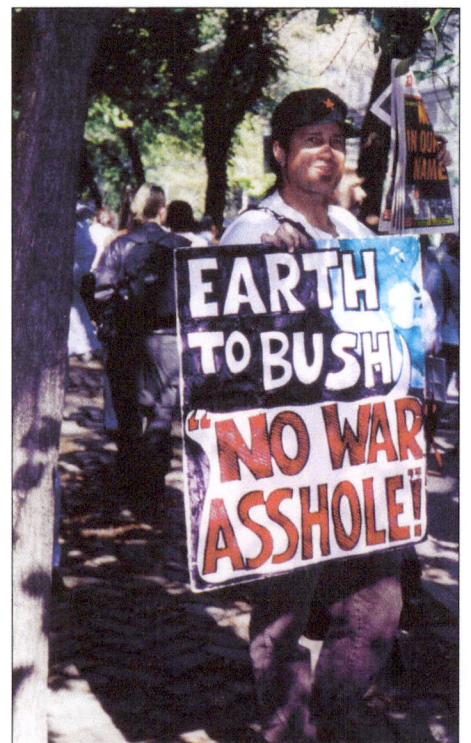

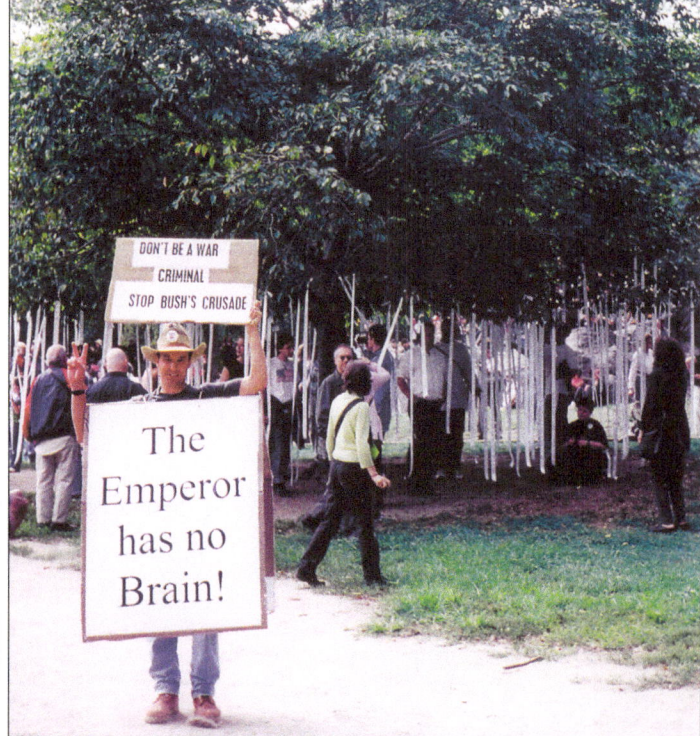

"Not in Our Name" war protest in Central Park, October 2002

against the Iraq war. During the *Global Day of Protest* hegemonic efforts were exacted on a federal level in the U.S. to obstruct and conceal resistance to the pending invasion. Authorities in America's largest cities brazenly defied the First Amendment of the U.S. constitution by preventing millions of citizens from gathering at central locations to publicly voice their dissent. In New York City, Mayor Bloomberg denied march permits for the *World Says 'No' to War* demonstration, along with a conveniently timed "Code Orange" terror alert that resulted in bridges being shut down and cross-borough trains being stalled. Despite a myriad of obstacles, over half a million people marched through the streets of New York City for a day of protest that would go down in history.[13]

The record-breaking turnout for the *World Says 'No' to War* demonstration was largely facilitated by outreach over the Internet. At this time the Internet became the primary communication technology used for alternative news reporting and protest organizing, and served as a central tool for building a strong grassroots coalition to counter the mass media's pro-war stance. It provided a platform for the voices that had been excluded from mainstream media, enabling ordinary people to broadcast ideas and information to the public. My participation in the *World Says 'No' to War* demonstration stemmed from an enticing email I received from Complacent.org (a politically-minded art collective) about a carnival protest party in conjunction to the demonstration and peace rally: "The planet feels perilous. Dissent is being denied. Violence is being offered as the only solution. You want to speak out, be heard and have fun doing it. This is your chance."

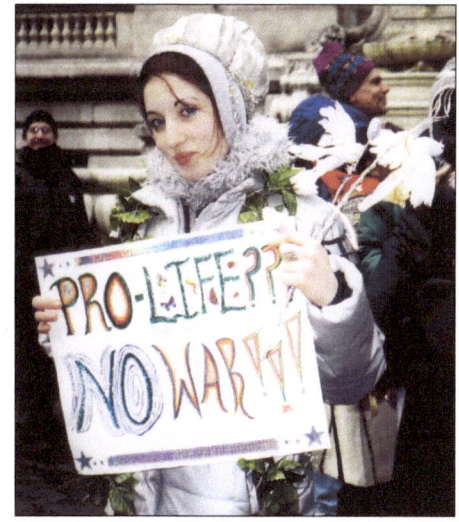

The carnival concept for the protest inspired me to design a silver sparkling "Princess for Peace" costume and a colorful "Pro-Life? NO War!!!" banner. I wanted to be adorned as a shining beacon of light, while my sign called attention to the hypocrisy and diversion tactics being employed by the Bush administration. Republicans had long spearheaded a morality campaign seeking to control women's reproductive rights by banning abortion – under the guise of saving the lives of unborn babies – while simultaneously lobbying to drop bombs on women and children overseas.

Princess for Peace, 2003

---

13   *The Global Day of Protest Against War on Iraq on Feb. 15th, 2003 was considered to be the largest global anti-war demonstration in the history of the world… Between 10-13 million people in over 600 cities voiced opposition to the Bush/Blair strike. These numbers are staggering considering the demonstration took place before the war had started (Lampord, 2004: 5).*

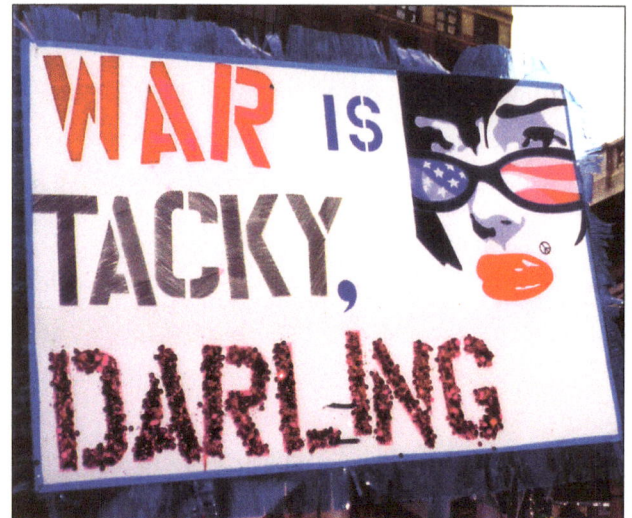

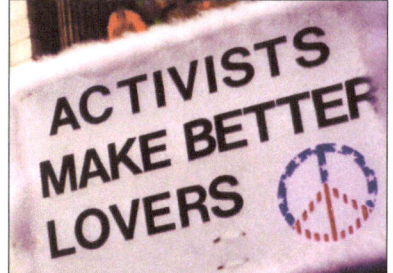

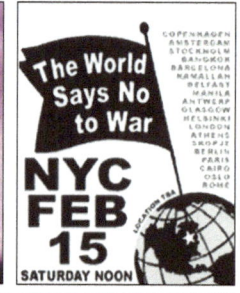

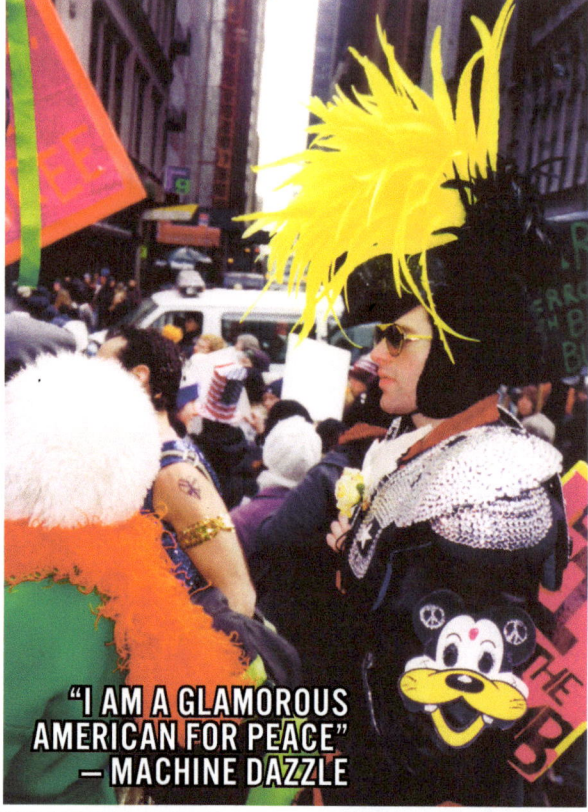

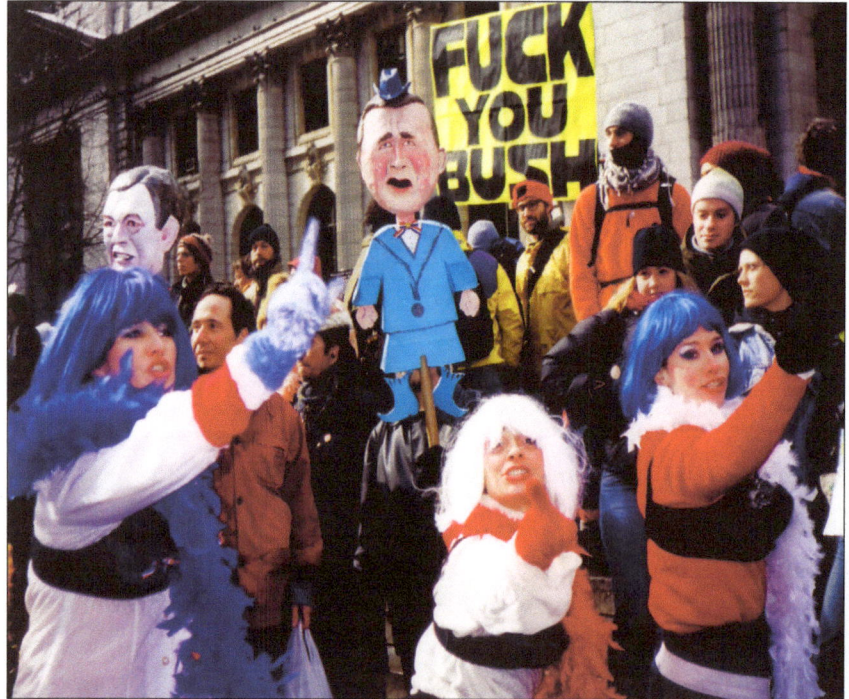

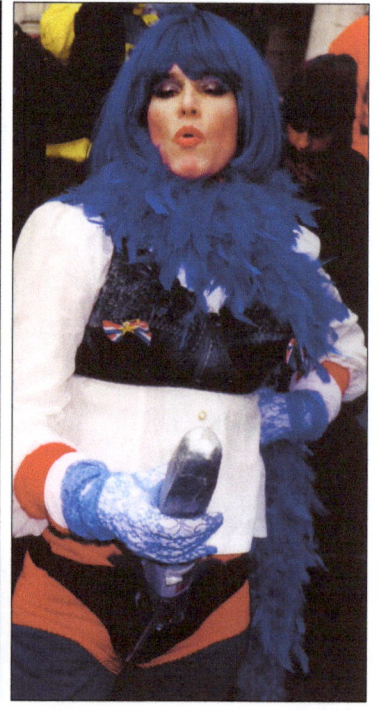

The Glam Americans and Missile Dick Chicks perform at the *World Says 'No' to War* demonstration, NYC, February 2003

Dressed to the luminescent nines, I arrived in midtown Manhattan to find the streets overflowing with protesters. Despite below freezing temperatures and lack of march permits, the turnout was larger than anyone had expected. I made my way over to the flamboyant carnival protest at the 42nd Street library. Information flyers were being distributed along with beads to encourage carnival solidarity. Cameras flashed as the fabulous "Glam Americans" and "Missile Dick Chicks" paraded about. The Missile Dick Chicks were a guerrilla theater troupe that parodied ladies from Texas while dancing and singing catchy jingles about American consumerism, war, and lust for oil. On the library steps, they belted out a song to the tune of the Supremes "Stop in the Name of Love" – "Shop in the name of war! You need a whole lot more, don't think it o-o-over! Without taxes on your consumer billions, Uncle Sam can't afford to bomb civilians!"

After attending the exuberant carnival at the library, I began to march with friends to the peace rally. The atmosphere quickly grew ominous. The sidewalks were becoming dangerously crowded as police officers on horseback intimidated demonstrators to stay off the street by threatening to make arrests and pushing into the crowd with their steeds. When we arrived at 3rd Avenue we were literally penned into the sidewalk, unable to advance to the peace rally on 1st Avenue. Judy Sky, an activist who had protested the Vietnam War, said to me: "The police are not going to let the anti-war contingency congregate in one place. They are using this tactic to divide us in order to downplay the magnitude of the demonstration, so there will appear to be fewer people when it is covered on the news. So much for progress, this is all a throw back to the 1960s."

The sidewalk march on 3rd Avenue crawled slowly toward the peace rally within the confines of the barricade. At each blocked off entrance the police would tell us to keep going, and that the next street would be open. Once I realized that the fuckery could go on forever, I decided to aggressively maneuver my way across the avenues. I slipped through the side door of a deli on 3rd Ave that allowed me to gain access to 2nd Ave, and then scurried around for nearly an hour trying to find an access point to the peace rally, but to no avail. The police would not budge. A woman with a group of young children tried to bargain with the officers at a barricade, "Please let us into the rally. I brought the children all the way from upstate New York, to teach them to exercise their rights." "Sorry lady," was the cop's callous response. Moments later, things began to get ugly on 2nd Ave. I witnessed police on horseback stampede and trample demonstrators trying to bypass the barricade to attend the peace rally. People, puppets, and signs were falling to the ground; arrests were being made all around. I swiftly ducked into a nearby doorway to avoid getting assaulted or arrested by the police.

PARADES, PARTIES, AND PROTESTS

After my failed attempt to attend the peace rally on 1st Avenue, I headed over to Times Square on 42nd Street where a makeshift protest was taking place. The police had formed a blockade so dense, there was no view of the activists participating in the demonstration. Wherever and however people tried to voice opposition to the Iraq war during the 2/15 *World Says 'No' to War* protest in New York City, they were met with forceful uniformed resistance. I left feeling defeated and depleted, mulling over the hypocrisy of so-called American democracy. Despite the overwhelming vocalization of dissent by millions of people in the U.S. and abroad, the Iraq war was officially launched on March 20th, 2003.

Two days after the initial U.S-led invasion of Iraq, on March 22nd, 2003, another large demonstration took place in New York City that was attended by over 300,000 people. It was a far less harrowing experience then the protest in February, with warmer weather, a friendlier police force, and march permits granted from 42nd Street to Washington Square Park. However, it was too little too late. The war had already begun, and thousands of people had been discouraged from participating in public displays of resistance due to the chaos and police brutality at the previous month's protest. Many suffered from deep-seated feelings of malaise and helplessness when confronted with the painful realization that we were all at the mercy of a nefarious government that blatantly ignored the outcries of its constituents.

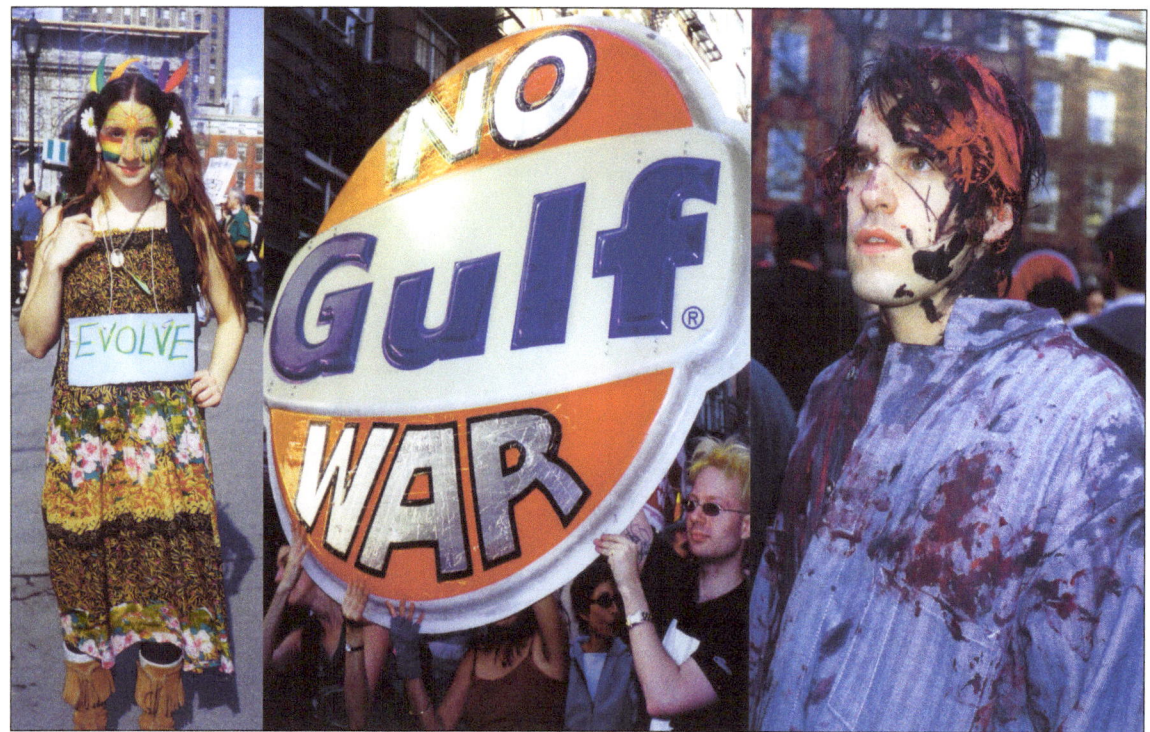

Iraq War protest at Washington Square Park, NYC, March 2003

38

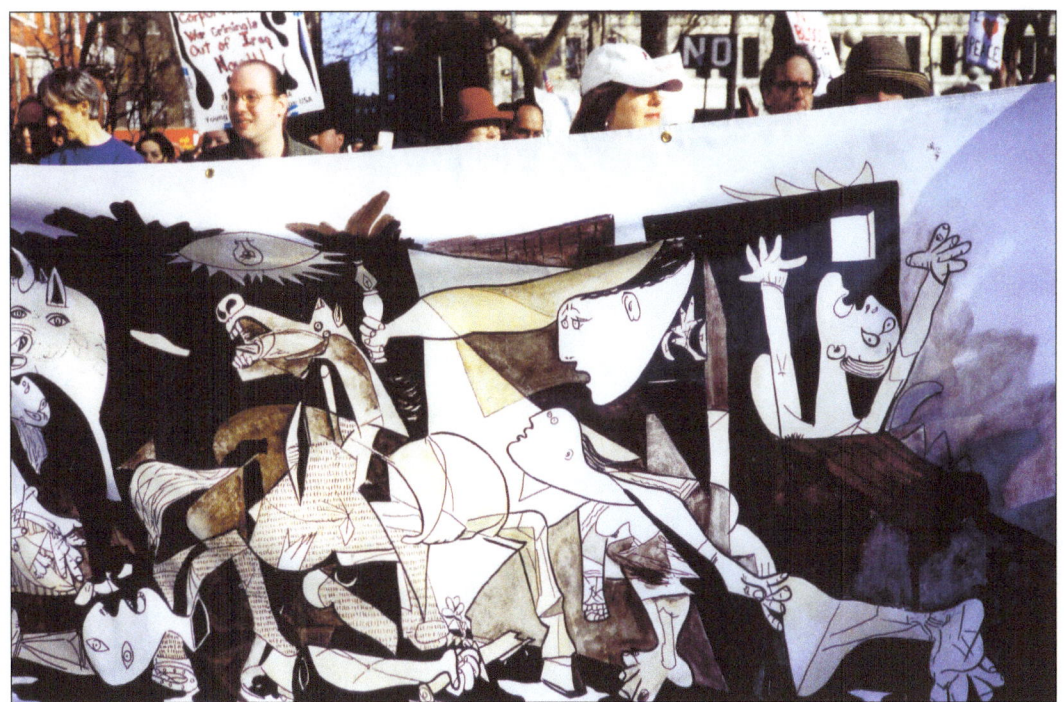

"Guernica" by Pablo Picasso – a universal symbol of resistance to war and fascism
Washington Square Park, NYC, March 2003

The demonstration in March culminated with a peace rally at Washington Square Park in the West Village. Many people attended the rally wearing evocative costumes; one blood-and-oil covered young man embodied Iraqi civilians, while a young woman adorned in Native American garb brandished a sign that read "EVOLVE." A group of demonstrators marched alongside the park holding a striking banner with large images taken from Pablo Picasso's "Guernica." The painting is one of the quintessential examples of art that was created as a tool to bear witness to tragedy and expose injustice. It is considered by many to be an icon that defines political art and is a universal symbol of resistance to war and fascism.[14]

In the months surrounding the record-breaking 2/15 *World Says 'No' To War* demonstration, more than ten million people around the globe came together in a unified effort to declare opposition to the Iraq invasion. While the whole world was watching, the President of the United States George W. Bush downplayed the impact of the largest, most creative global mobilizations for peace in history by saying he couldn't base his decisions on "a focus group" (Purdum, 2003).

---

14 *On April 26th, 1937 the Basque town of Guernica was destroyed by German bombers flying for General France; in less than a week Picasso began his painting Guernica. It is thought to be a continuous protest against the brutality of fascism in particular and modern war in general. For millions of people now, the name of Guernica accuses all war criminals and might be a protest against a massacre of the innocents at any time (Berger, 1965: 164).*

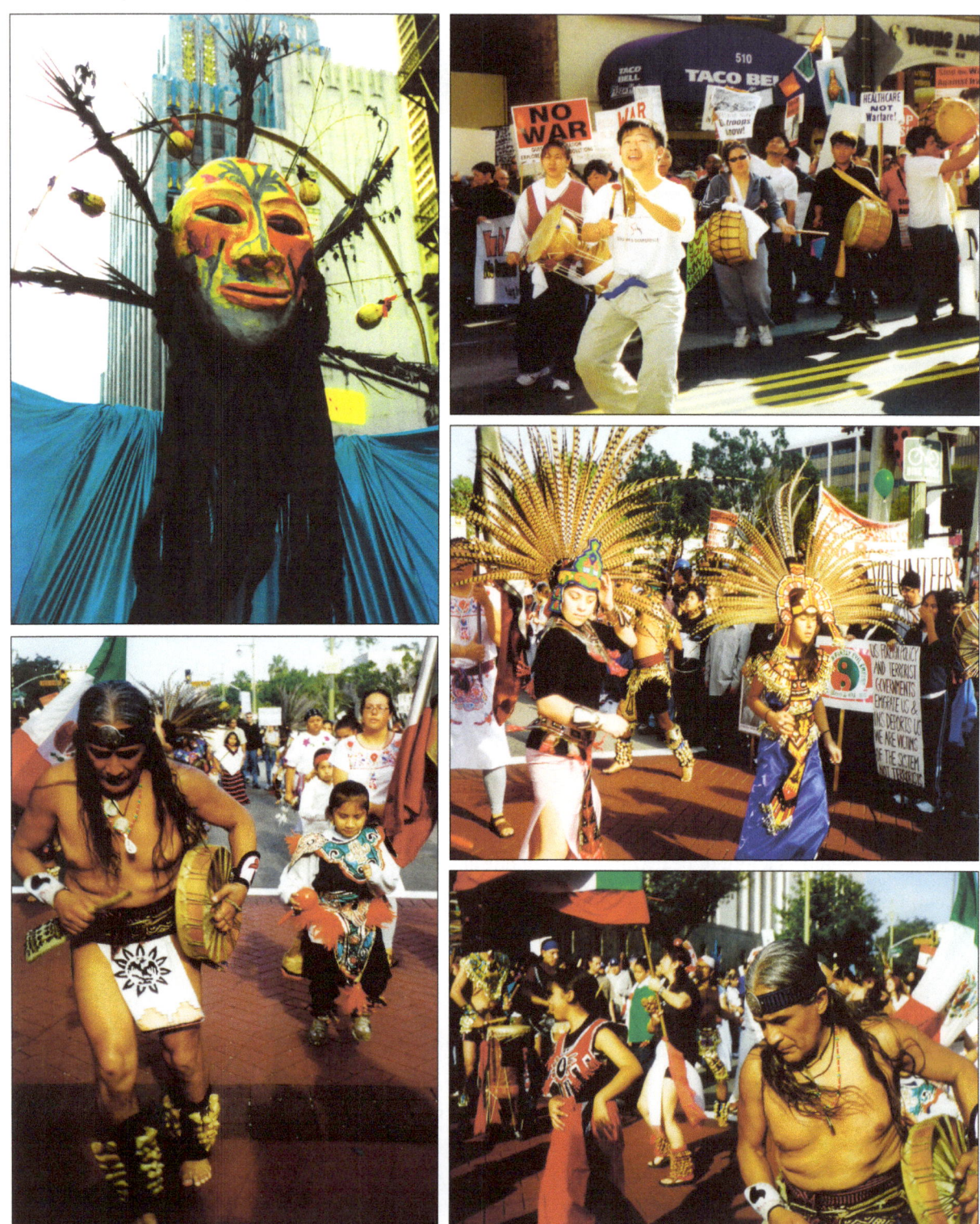

Visual art and performance at Iraq war protest in Downtown Los Angeles, January 2003

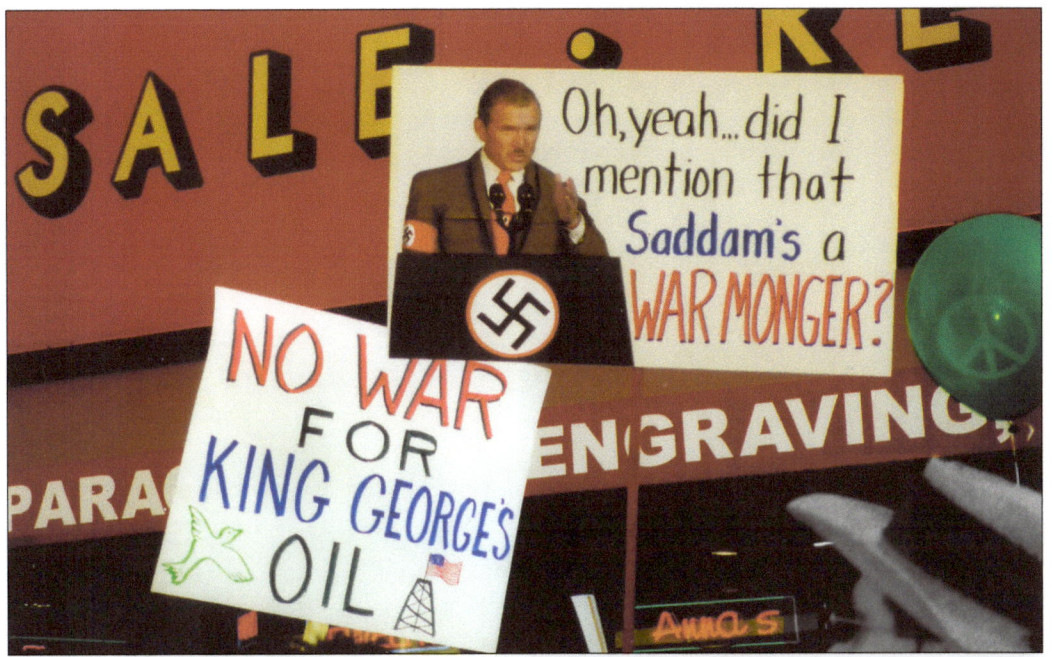

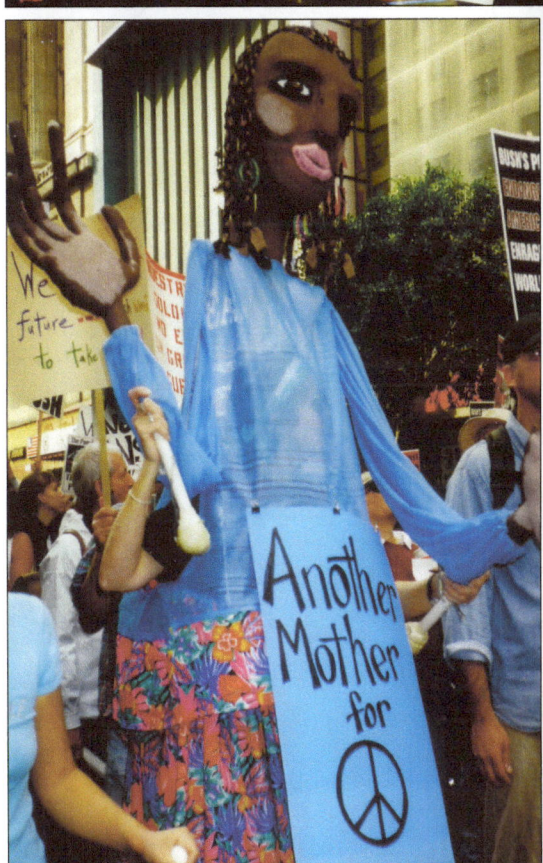

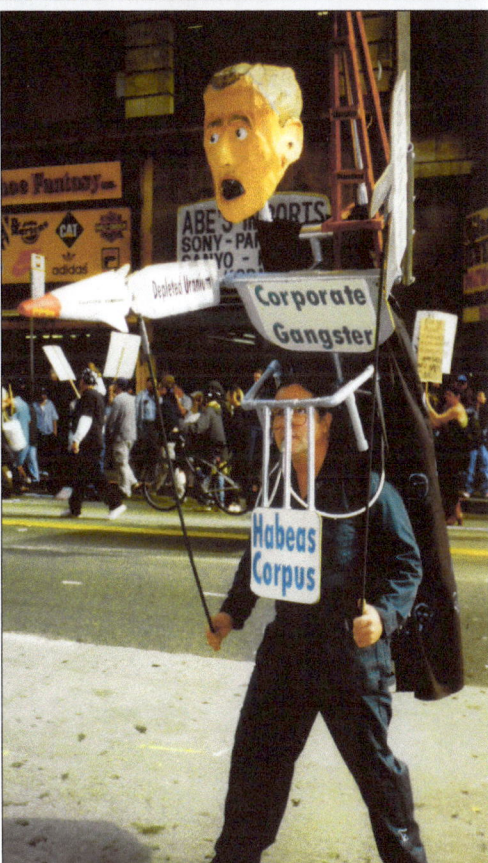

Puppets and classic signage from Los Angeles' largest preemptive war protest in history, January 2003

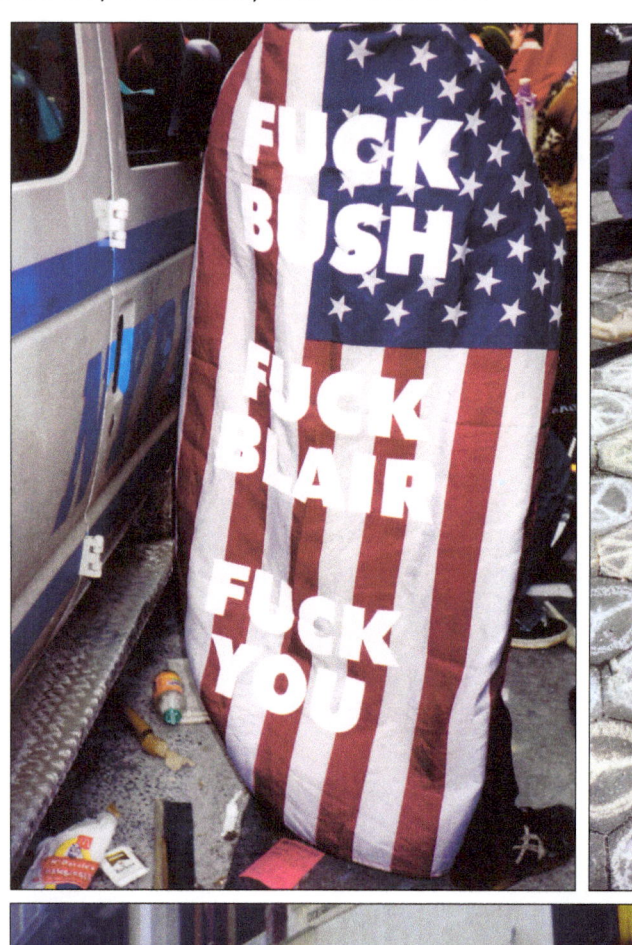

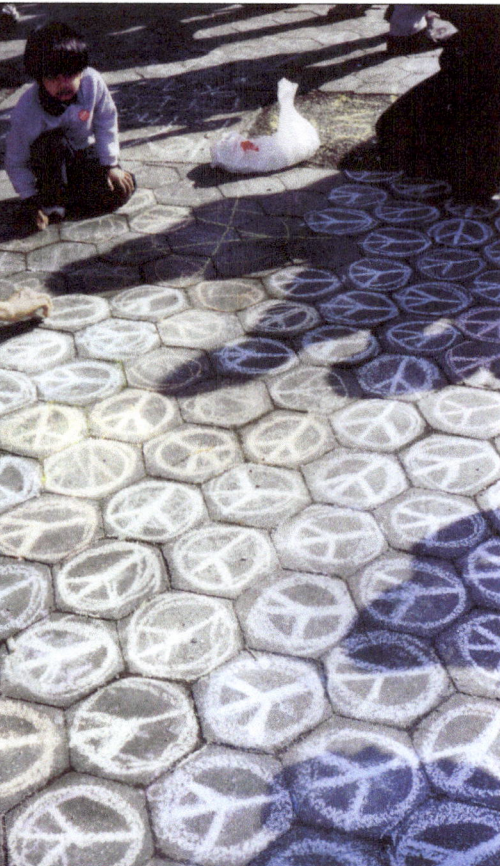

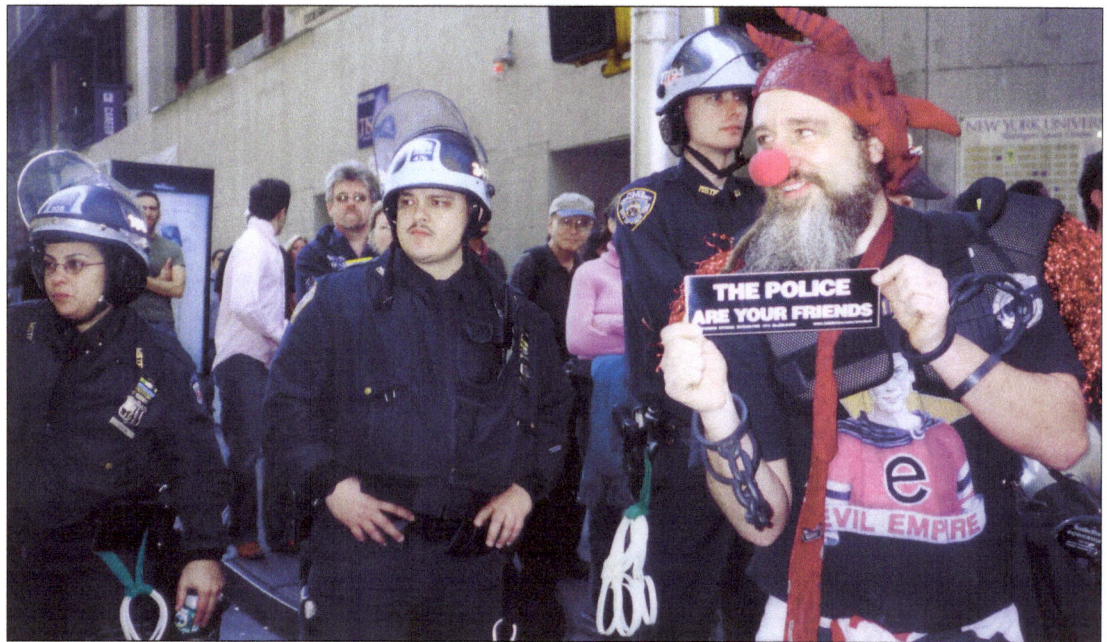

"The Police Are Your Friends," *The World Still Says 'No' to War* demonstration, NYC, March 2003

New York Says 'No' to War

February 15, 2003

The powers that be
Shrouded in hypocrisy
Lies in disguise
As democracy.

They don't want the world to see
The capacity
Of the anti-war contingency.
March permits denied
 In New York City.
On hyper terror alert
For the peace rally.

Roadblocks for miles around,
The talk of the town.
Dissent must be kept at bay,
Trains stalled
To keep the masses away.

Freezing cold, but not alone.
Half a million protesters
Chilled to the bone.
"Whose streets? Our streets!"
Beating on drums
And stamping the feet.

In opposition to
The white house resident,
A cowboy president.

The "focus group" coup
Fenced in like cattle.
Amidst the panic and fear,
"Drop Bush Not Bombs!" they cheer.

I burst into tears,
When I could go no further,
Protesting government inflicted hysteria
And war fervor.
Denied access
To the peace rally,
And my American right of
Freedom of assembly.

At the barricades
Pepper was sprayed.
Peaceful people
Were dragged away.
Police horses stampede
Women and children bleed
On Second Avenue and in Iraq.

Rally for peace
Turned into a day of turmoil
While protesting a government
Wanting to reap the spoils
Of a Middle Eastern nation
Abundant in oil.

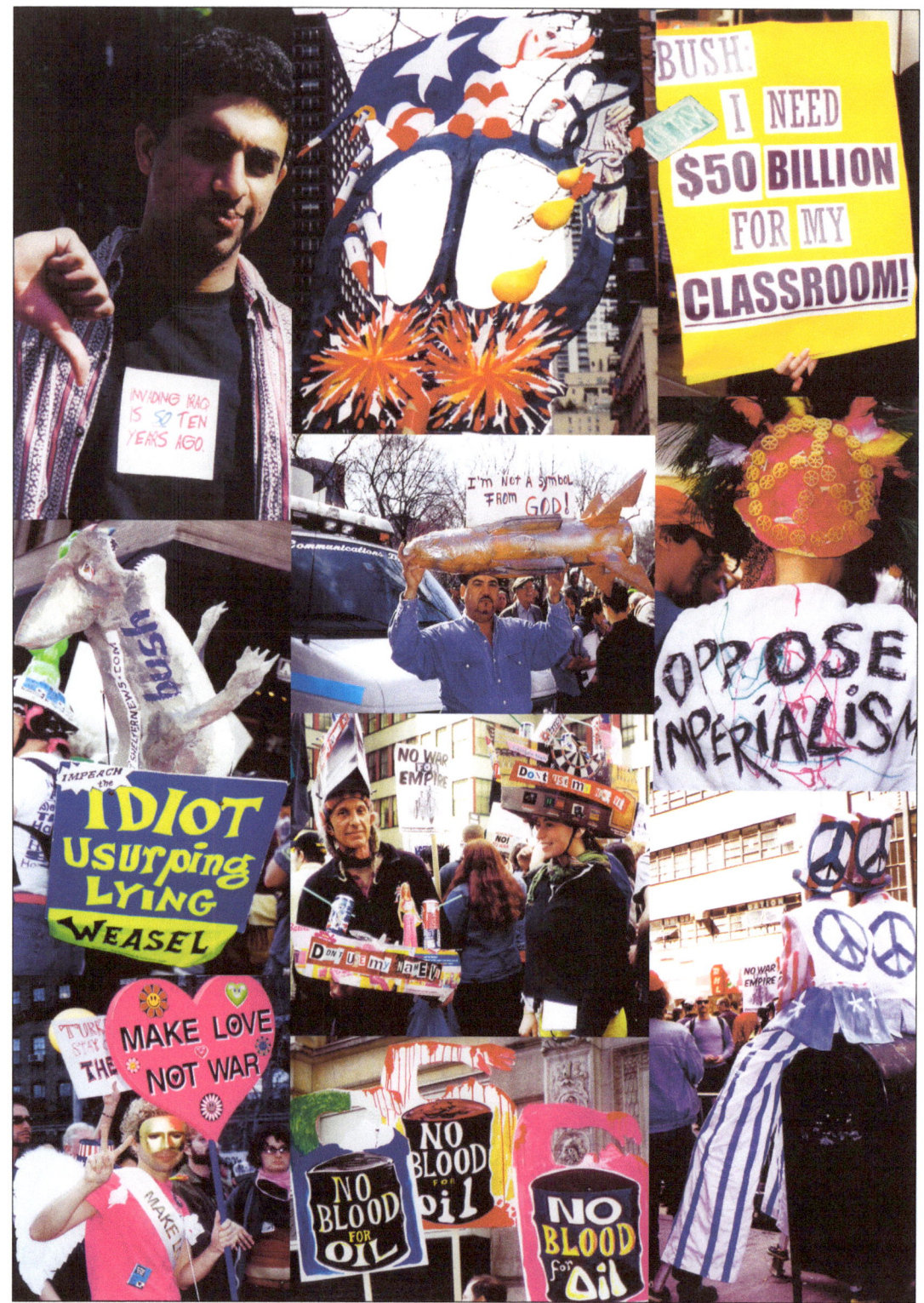

"Make Art, Not War!" creative resistance in New York City, 2003

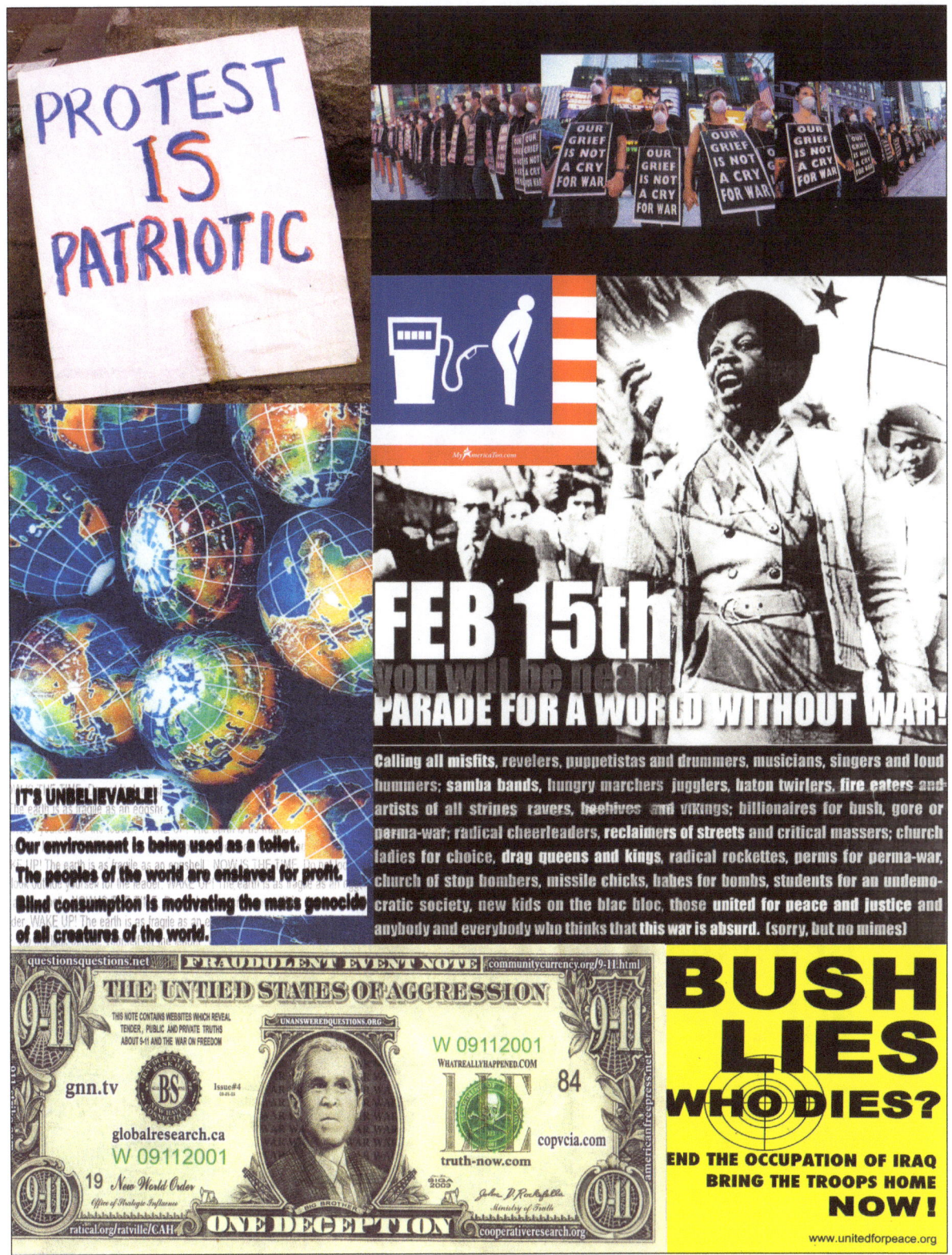

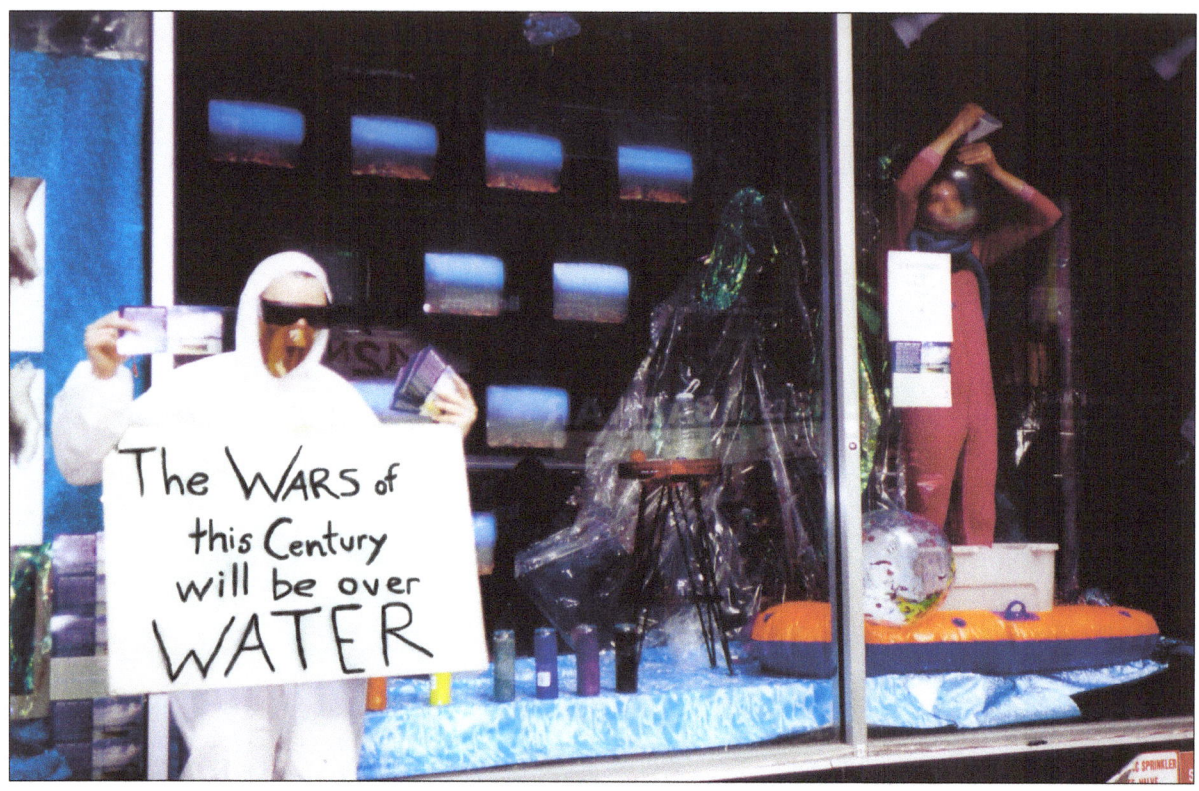

"The Wars of This Century Will Be Over Water" – Performance art by Michael Kane and Mangina
Water Water Festival at the Chashama Theatre, NYC, 2003

" THE WARS OF THIS CENTURY WILL BE OVER WATER "

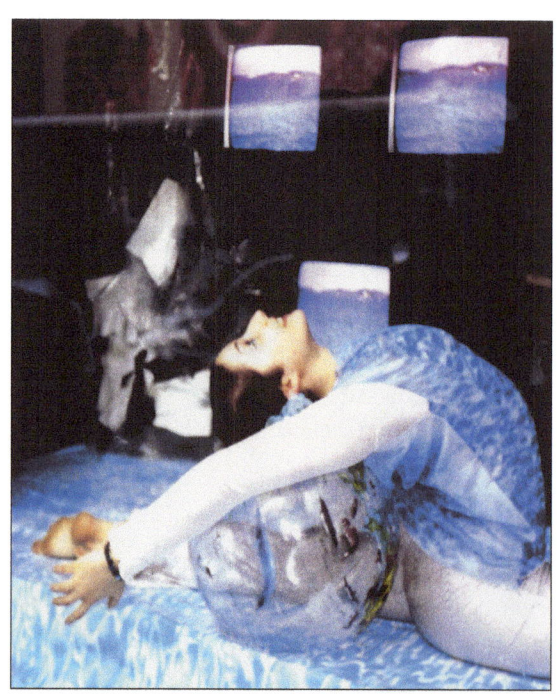

"Ocean Contortion" by Sarah Sparkles
Water Water Festival, 2003

THE WATER
WATER FESTIVAL
MARCH 16-23, 2003

During that fateful week in March 2003, while the U.S. teetered on the brink of war with Iraq, a collaborative multi-media ecology festival called "Water Water" was held in New York City. Water Water was designed to raise awareness about the impending crisis of fresh water scarcity at a time when critical global environmental concerns were being ignored during the march to war. Amidst the frenetic consumer mecca of 42nd Street, the Water Water festival applied an Agitprop technique known as "Artivism" (art + activism) to provide outreach to people who are not normally exposed to information about water conservation. According to the festival's organizer Missy Galore: "We are treating Water Water as a festival of hope, to help people appreciate what they have and learn why they need to work to protect it. Water consciousness today is peace medicine for the future. The fact that war for oil came up this week is ironic because water is a resource that is more vital to our existence. The inspiration for this event derives from Pete Seeger being instrumental in getting the Hudson River cleaned up, and the example of artists before me that were using art as a medium for the social good."

The Water Water festival at the Chashama Theater on 42nd Street cultivated a powerful artistic platform to advocate for the conservation, and sustainable management of fresh water. Throughout the week, the sidewalk and theater window displays were transformed into a podium showcasing performances celebrating water as the planet's most valuable natural resource. Singers, fire-spinners, contortionists, and theatrical performance artists all took to the stage to share their unique H_2O-inspired creations. As the performers inside the windows were introduced, informational flyers were distributed on the street and speeches were made addressing water pollution and privatization. The festival sought to attract the public's attention with art, provide education, and garner community involvement surrounding a crucial, yet critically understated environmental concern.

PARADES, PARTIES, AND PROTESTS

The Water Water Festival in New York City was produced in conjunction to the World Water Forum in Kyoto, Japan, where global business leaders were holding a summit to address the pressing need to improve the quality and quantity of fresh water available to future generations. The Water Water festival hosted a teleconference with the forum in Kyoto to inform the general public about the issues at hand and encourage them to actively participate in the political process. The festival combined education with activism to empower people to make informed decisions and come up with proactive strategies for making lifestyle choices that support fresh water conservation. The educational focus of the Water Water festival echoed that of AIDS awareness organization ACT-UP that was formed in the late 1980s. ACT-UP members successfully obtained greater access to AIDS medication and more affordable treatment by becoming highly educated on their cause and finding compelling ways to impart that knowledge on the public.[15]

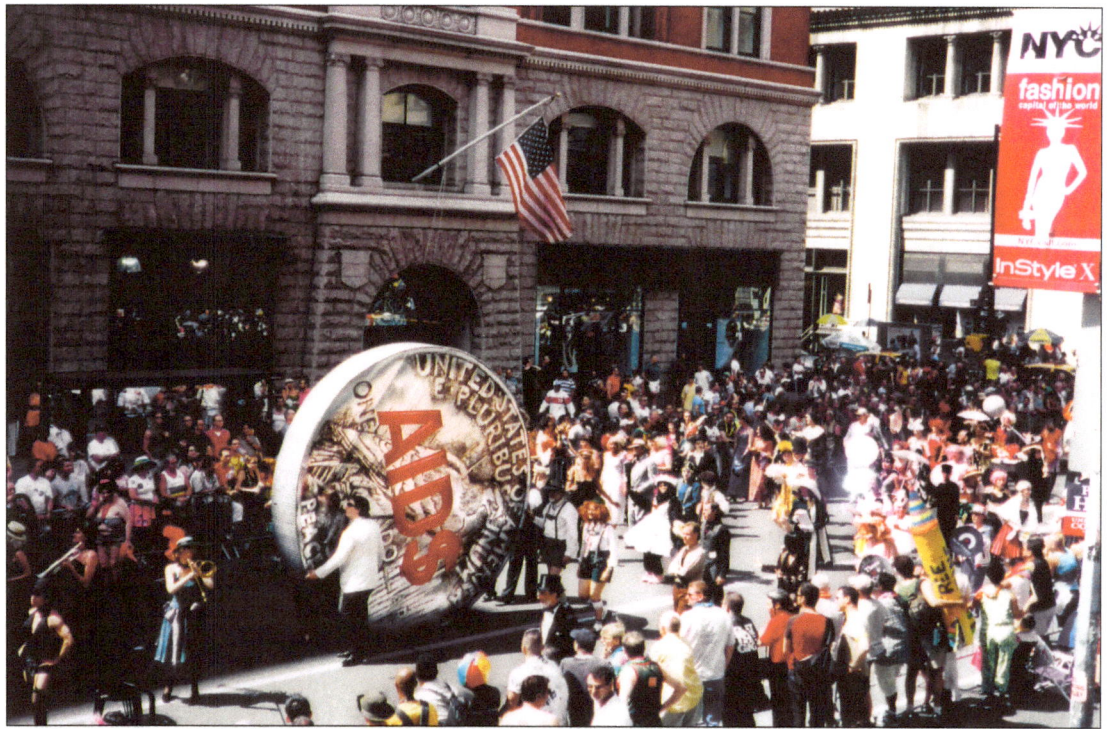

AIDS funding procession at the Gay Pride parade in NYC, 2004

---

15 *"We taught ourselves to become experts, to enable us to answer reporter's questions and to debate successfully with government and scientific officials. We learned that it helped to advance our cause when we were able to suggest workable solutions to the problems we were protesting ... We also learned to have lawyers present at all demonstrations to guard against police abuse ... Videotaping of demonstrations also helped prevent police abuse and win court cases" (Sawyer, 2002: 91).*

The Water Water Festival – March 16-23, 2003

The Water Water festival served as a vital channel for community building during troubled times, engaging artists and activists in an uplifting act of collective creation. After a week of spirited performances and town hall meetings, the festival ended on a more somber note. On March 20th, 2003, the day the Iraq war officially began, I attended the auspiciously timed Spring Equinox Peace Bell Ceremony at the United Nations that coincided with the finale of the Water Water Festival and the U.N. International Year of Fresh Water. In the courtyard of this hallowed international epicenter, a towering Peace Bell encased by a Shinto pagoda stood elegantly inside a delicately manicured garden. I found solace and solidarity amongst an environmentally conscious community at this unexpected sanctuary in the middle of a city throbbing with tension and anxiety during the onset of war. Just before the bell tolled, there was a moment of silent, focused intention as brave citizens held a torch for preservation of the Earth's natural resources and universal love. The silence was finally broken by the gong of the bell reverberating into the night. Everything has an echo; ours was a prayer for peace.

Open Your Eyes

Open your eyes

and read between the lies.

The poison that makes the world go round

will be our demise.

Televisions left on

'til the crack of dawn

while down the hall, or at the mall ...

We don't learn and it burns,

then we wonder why

it's December, but it feels like July.

We throw it away

day after day

bottles and cans

and the future of man, kind?

A toxic trail left behind.

Freshkills landfill closes

but what no one knows is

their backyard is next.

Who has the resolve

to dissolve

the denial

of a lifestyle

that is the bane of their own existence?

Human Nature

In the earliest days
  since the dawn of time
people prayed to the spirits of
plants, animals, and stones.
  They gave thanks.

  The earth was
mother, provider, sacred home.
  Everything was earth.
    Every One.

Until:

Highways paved over
natural consciousness.
Earth Mother was sold
to the highest bidder.
Her orphaned children,
left to fend for themselves.
Prey to corporate wolves,
hungry and greedy
for wealth.

The result:

  Waste lands.
  A landscape littered with
      weapons of mass destruction
        pumping poison
from tail pipes and smoke stacks
and it goes
      back
    back
      back
to the air we breath
      the food we eat
        the water we drink.

        Cancer
      Depression
      Addiction
      Bi-polar
    It even effects
The way we treat each other.

Who took
the human
Out of nature?

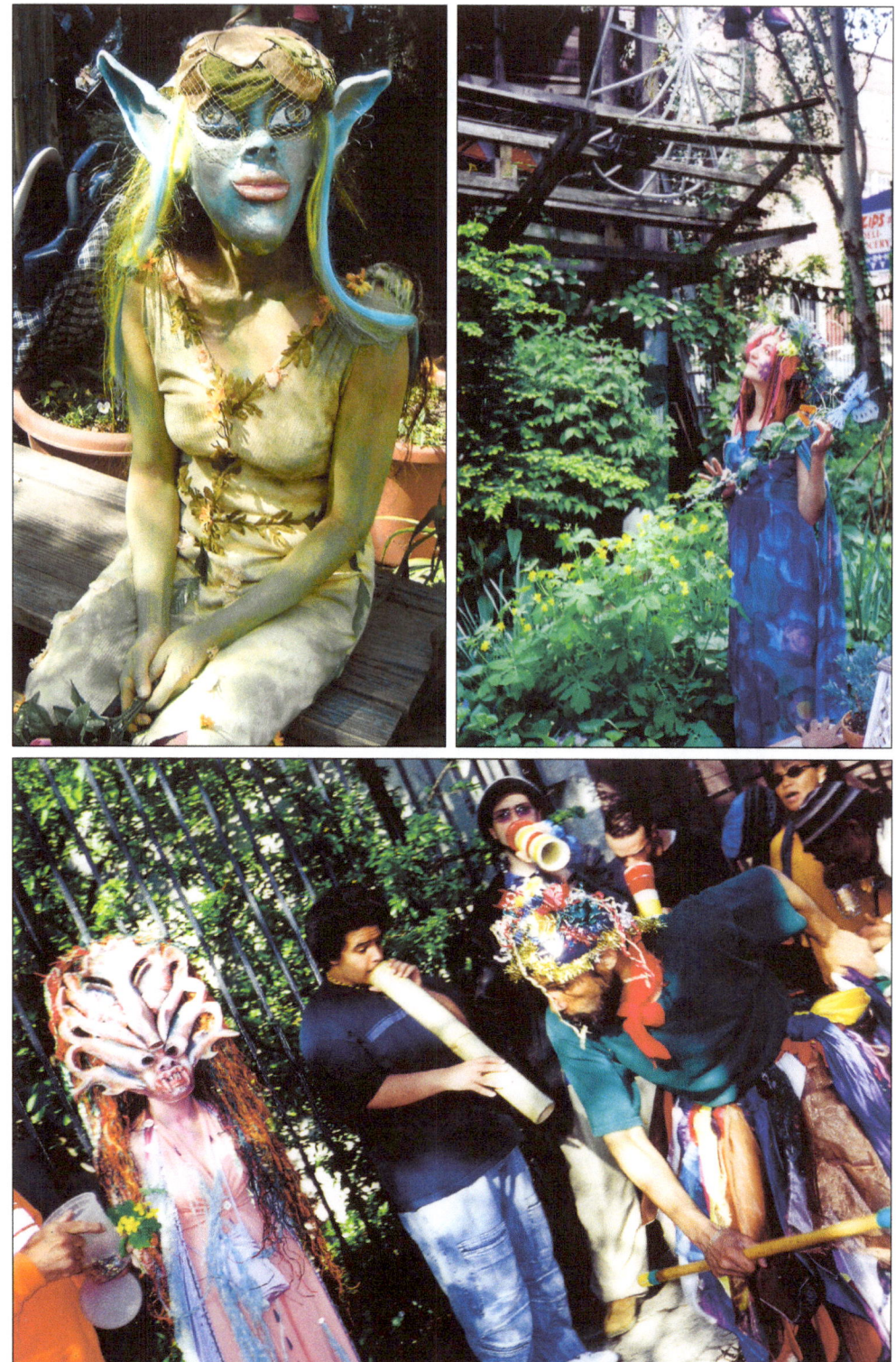

Garden faries and community ritual at the Rites of Spring Pageant, NYC, 2005

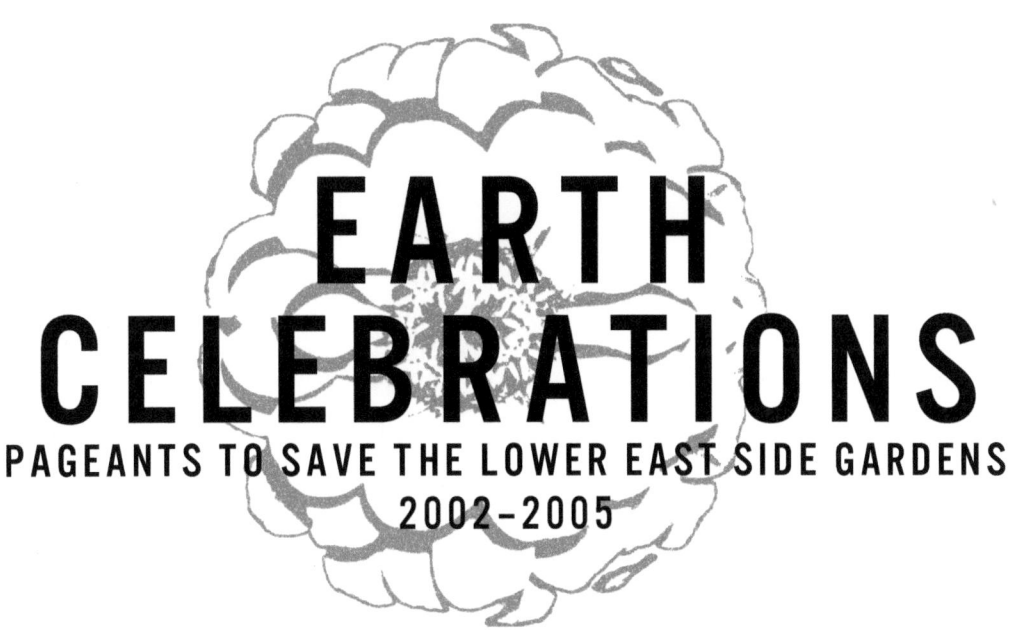

EARTH CELEBRATIONS

PAGEANTS TO SAVE THE LOWER EAST SIDE GARDENS
2002–2005

On a glorious spring afternoon in New York City, a procession of jewel-encrusted mythical creatures engulf the streets of the Lower East Side. Satyrs, shamans, and fairies dance in the streets to a melodic symphony of bells, drums, and horns. In their midst, performers in white march solemnly, bearing a mobile shrine to the elements. A young man covered from head to toe in verdant foliage greets awestruck bystanders and invites them to join the festivities. "It's a community celebration, everyone is welcome!" the Green Man proclaims. The procession enters a lush garden on 6th Street, where people are playing guitar and reciting poetry while volunteers serve plates of bread, cheese, and fruit. A costumed honeybee and sunflower perform a pollination dance alongside a vegetable patch. As the spectacle draws to a close, a bright blue butterfly announces that the parade will be moving to a larger community garden a few blocks away. Hundreds of enchanted forest creatures and intrigued newcomers mobilize onto the street and reconvene at La Plaza Cultural. Upon arrival, a shaman blows his horn, sending a deep hush over the crowd. The sweet smell of sage wafts through the air as nymphs on fabric silks suspend and contort from weeping willow trees. A towering princess on stilts in a sparkling pink gown enters the garden and sings a spellbinding opera. The crowd is transfixed, captivated by the magic of the annual Rights of Spring Pageant to save the Lower East Side gardens.

Founded in 1991 by Felicia Young, Earth Celebrations is a not-for-profit organization dedicated to promoting ecological awareness and community building through the arts. Earth Celebrations produced the annual collaboration of artists, activists, and gardeners that culminated twice a year with the daylong Rites of Spring and Winter Pageants. Marked by ornate costumes and puppetry that reflected a deep, Earth-based spirituality and animistic mythos, the pageants honored life cycles governed by seasonal change and paid homage to the sanctuary gardens provide from the chaos of city life. The creative and spiritual outpouring

53

at the pageants cultivated rich cultural experiences that instilled pride and honor in the community and a renewed sense of social responsibility for stewardship of the natural world.

The Rites of Spring Pageant was an annual, daylong, multi-cultural festival that toured a network of fifty Lower East Side Gardens. During the pageants, the gardens overflowed with music, storytelling, and theatrical performance. Many elements of theater and ritual were combined, including drumming, dancing, chanting, elaborate costumes, ceremonial art objects, and prayer. The pageants generated profound performances intertwined with ancient myths and symbolism while simultaneously addressing critical environmental issues and honoring the local history of the Lower East Side. The pageants told the stories of the garden's struggle to survive in New York City and of their preservation through diligent, unified community efforts.

During the 1970s, New York City's Lower East Side resembled a war zone, a bleak urban landscape of dilapidated tenement houses, vacant lots, and burnt-out buildings. When the housing market crashed, many landlords torched their properties to collect insurance money, leaving block-long stretches of rubble in their wake. The abandoned lots became demoralizing cesspools, squalid breeding grounds for the crime and drugs that had overrun the neighborhood. The city's authorities neglected the plight of the community, so the citizens of the Lower East Side took matters into their own hands. They rolled up their sleeves and began to clear out the rubble. In the following decade, residents transformed dozens of abandoned buildings into cherished homes, and garbage-

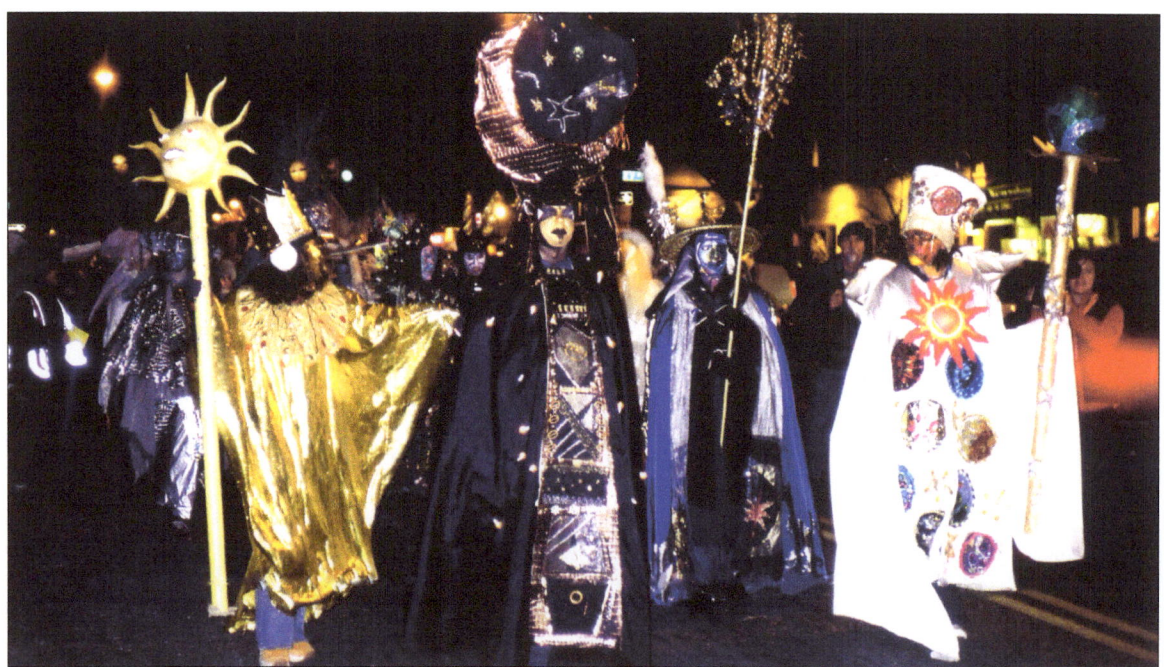

Earth Celebrations Winter Pageant, New York City, 2002

strewn lots into illustrious gardens. The gardens became community jewels that provided a lush natural oasis and served as venues for an array of exciting multi-cultural events.

As the Lower East Side became a more attractive neighborhood, real-estate developers hungrily sought to acquire the community gardens in order to demolish them and pave the way for luxury housing. The trend of gentrification with an iron fist took hold, with developers showing total disregard for those inhabiting up-and-coming locations. One of the many profound losses that occurred was the ill-fated demise of the Esperanza Community Garden, a cherished green sanctuary that was birthed by local residents in 1977. Esperanza was home to a thriving ecosystem of plants, small animals, community celebrations, and grassroots public theater. This vibrant community garden was bulldozed after the land was purchased from the city by an avaricious real estate developer Donald Cappocia, who had donated more money than was legally allowed to Mayor Giuliani's election campaign (Mikalbrown, 2002: 230). The Esperanza Garden was one of many

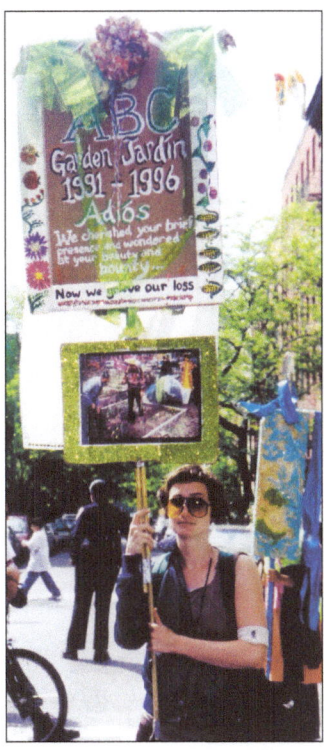

Effigies to lost gardens at the Rites of Spring Pageant, 2003

urban sanctuaries obliterated by the insatiable greed that is systematically eroding the soul of New York City – pricing out its natives, its nature, and its artists. In the face of adversity, community members created the Earth Celebrations Pageants to protest the real estate developers who wanted to destroy these treasured green public spaces and pay tribute to the community gardens that had already been lost in the name of "progress."

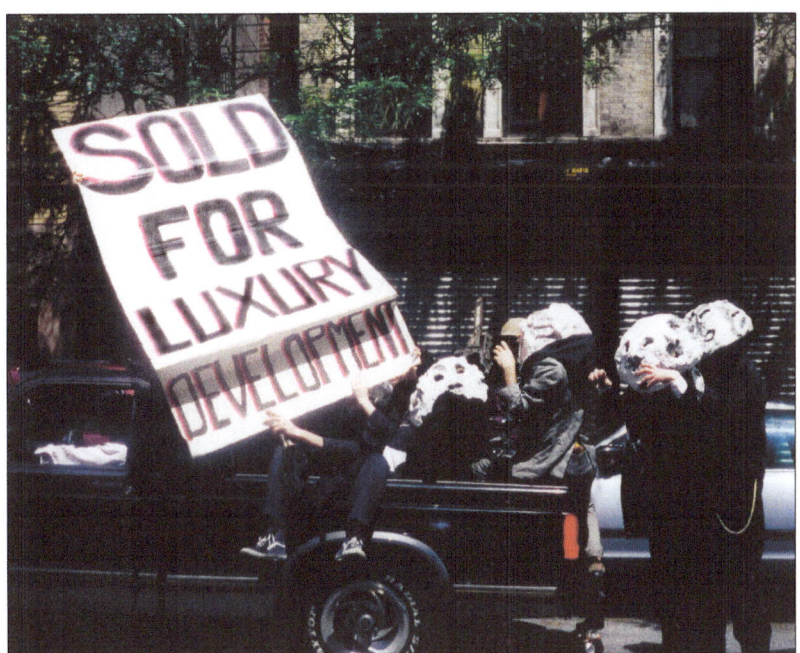

"Sold For Luxury Development:" Gentrification protest staged at the Earth Celebrations Pageant to save the Lower East Side gardens, 2002

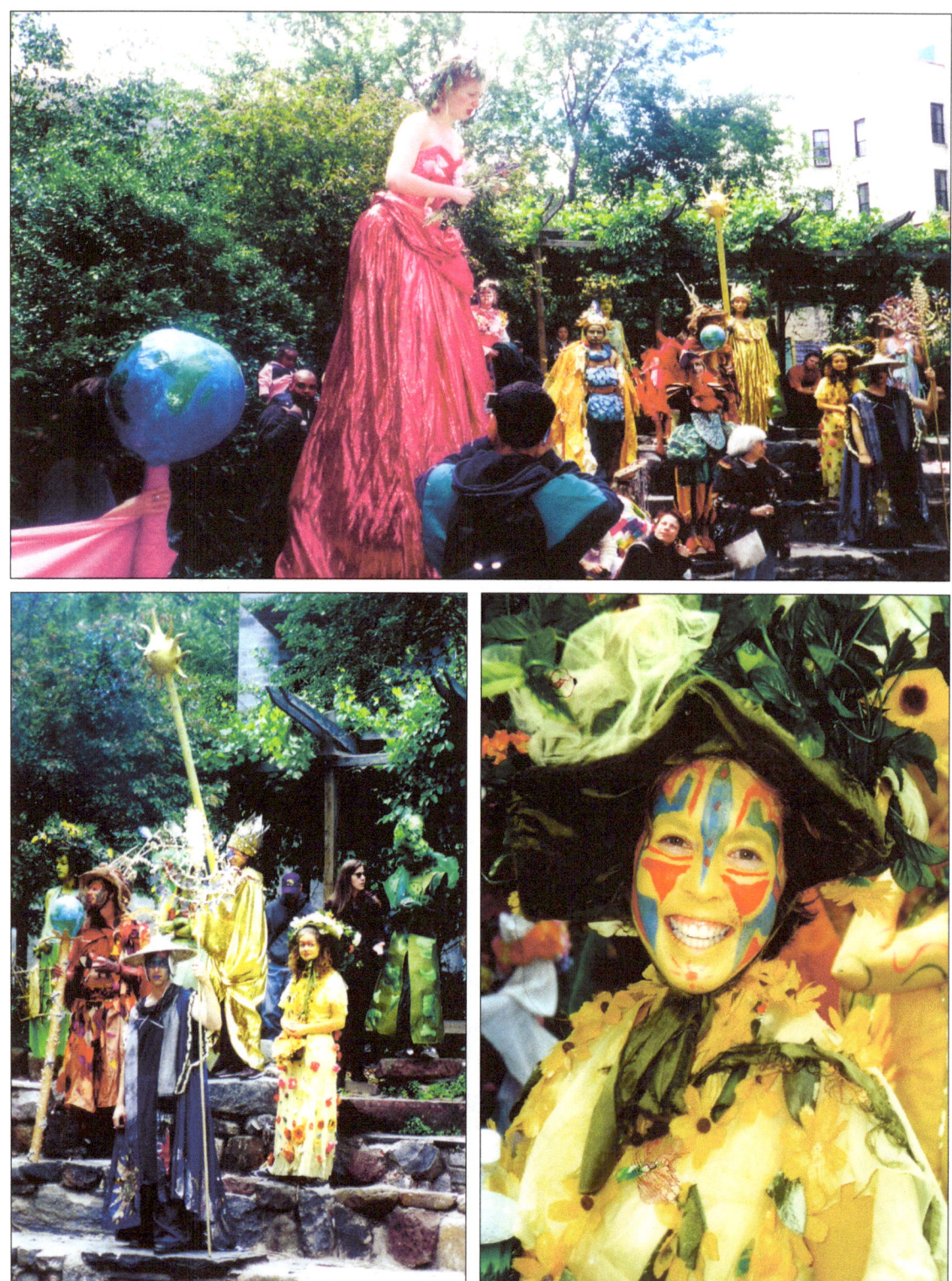

Earth Celebrations Rites of Spring Pageant at La Plaza Cultural, NYC, 2002

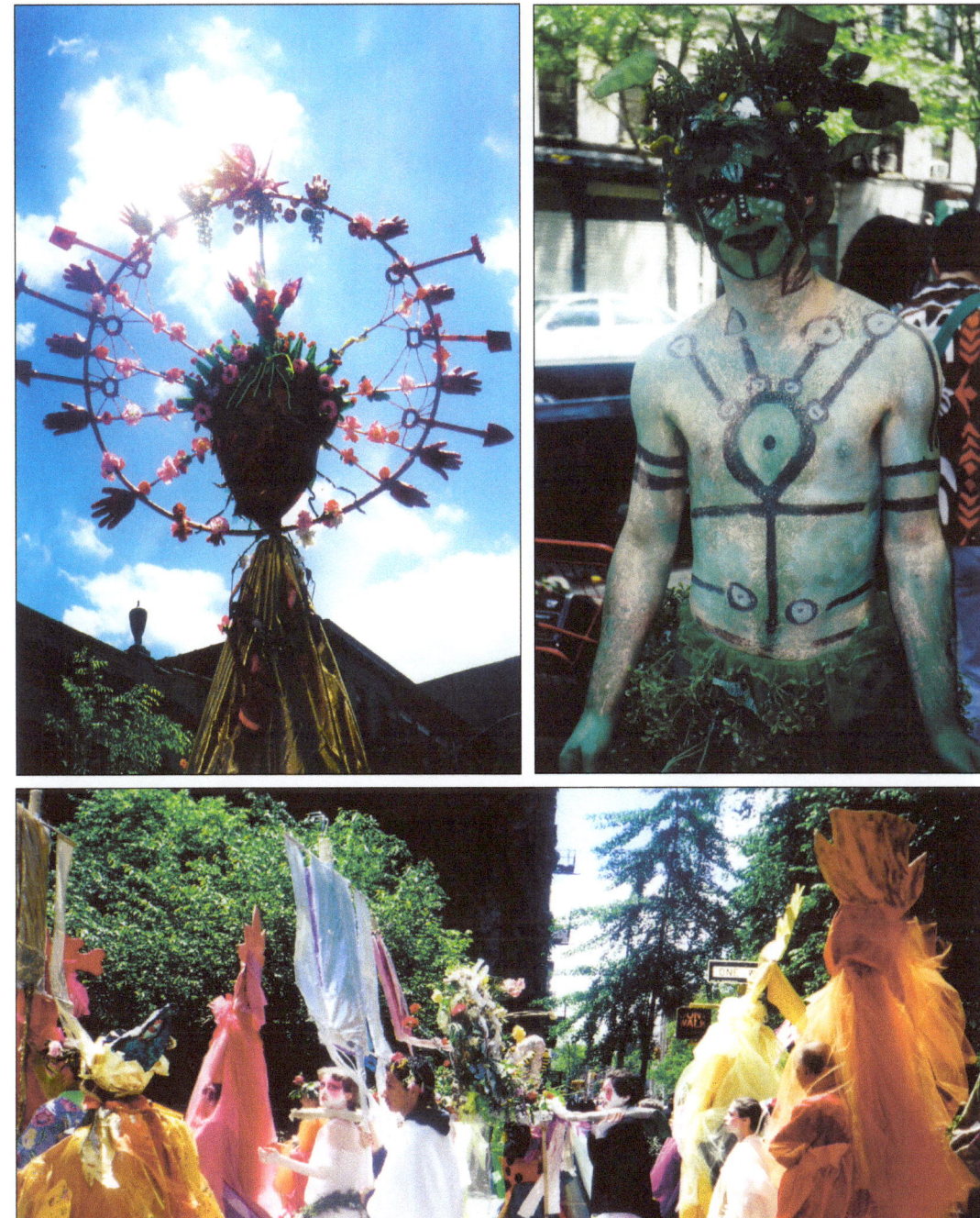

Rites of Spring procession, Lower East Side, 2002

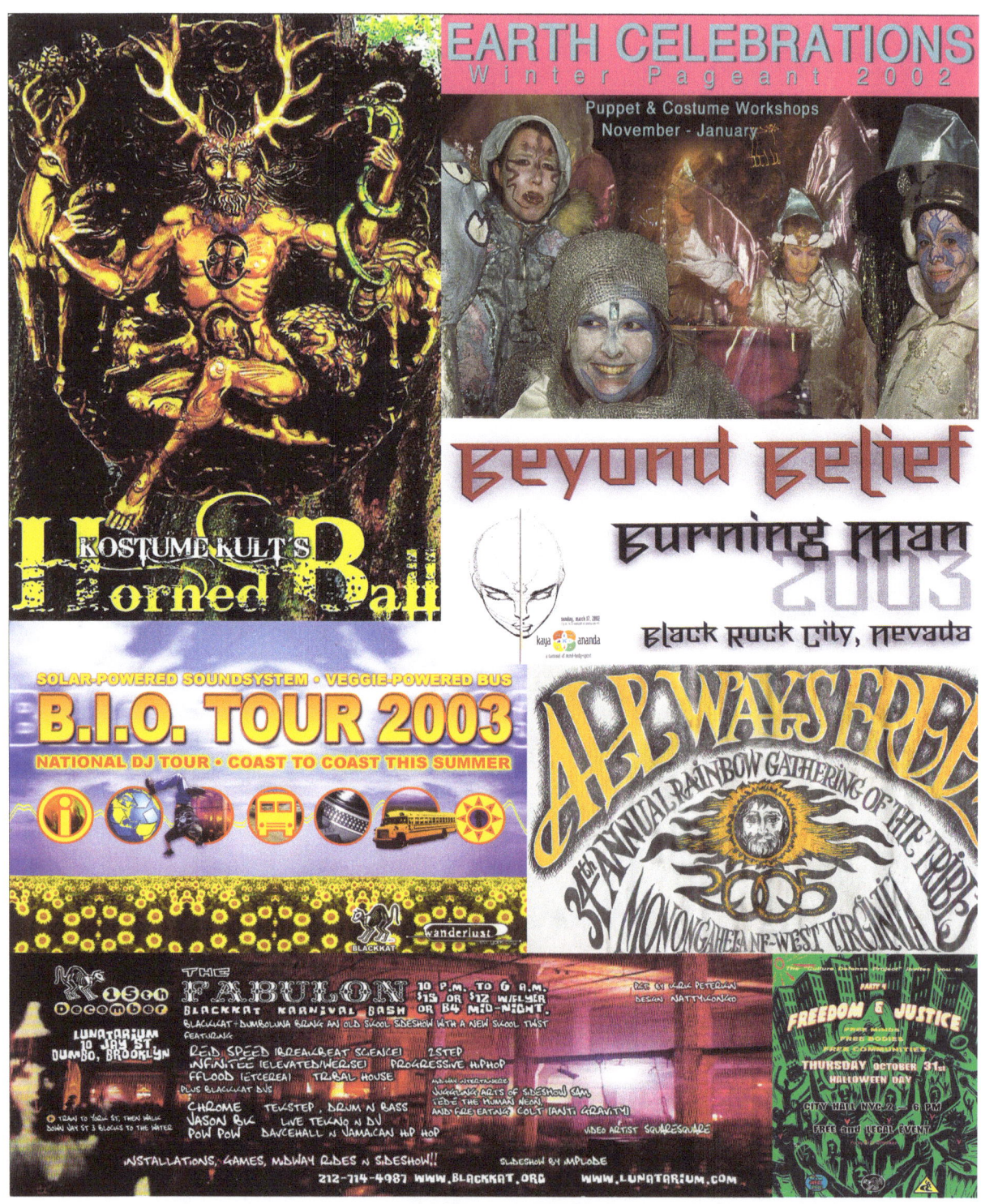

Party fliers, 2001-2005

UTOPIAN COMMUNITY CELEBRATIONS

Utopian celebrations challenge mainstream culture's claim to authority by offering an alternative paradigm that merges reality with desire. The element of transformation is omnipresent: as a dilapidated warehouse morphs into an art gallery, a vintage speakeasy cabaret, a cavernous metallic landscape that rivals outer space, or a three-ring circus where the lines between the spectacle and the audience are completely blurred. The subversion of the mundane is celebrated as renegade marching bands, break-dancers with boom boxes, and stilt-walkers spill into subway cars and onto city streets. Entrenched identities built upon the notions of race, gender, career, and class are transcended when riding around the desert on a pirate ship, or watching the sunrise from atop an art deco pyramid after a night of dancing under the stars. It is in these divine, surreal moments that we are reminded that anything is possible and we experience true liberation.

Characterized by openness and freedom, utopian gatherings push the boundaries of commonplace reality. Sanctioned social norms are cast aside in exchange for ecstatic revelry, community solidarity, and the transformation of conventional public spaces into unorthodox playing fields. Spectacles intertwined with mythical rituals are intrinsic to many of these events, inviting participants to explore uncharted creative, political, and spiritual dimensions. Collaborative community efforts are essential to the creation of utopian festivities. All-hands-on-deck initiatives are required to set up a massive warehouse party or build a makeshift city for a music festival in the depths of the jungle, the desert, or the woods. Operating within a D.I.Y. paradigm involves intense work, however the experience is often accompanied by a sense of ownership, camaraderie and satisfaction that cannot be purchased with an admission fee. These dynamic grassroots events cultivate legacies as people bond through working and playing together, embracing the freedom to turn their collective imaginations into reality.

During the post-9/11 Bush years, Utopian events boldly contrasted with the overtly political nature of Agitprop protests and somber Witness art mediums. Sans puppets emulating pompous politicians or faux bloodstained accoutrement worn in homage to the casualties of war, Utopian celebrations invoked empowering alternative realities and inspired hope for a better world. Warehouse parties transformed raw urban industrial spaces into whimsical dreamscape environments for showcasing avant-garde artists while offering an array of decadent late-night cavorting. The "One Night of Fire" circus-style street parties brought temporary liberation to the streets of New York where the grind of daily life is endured.

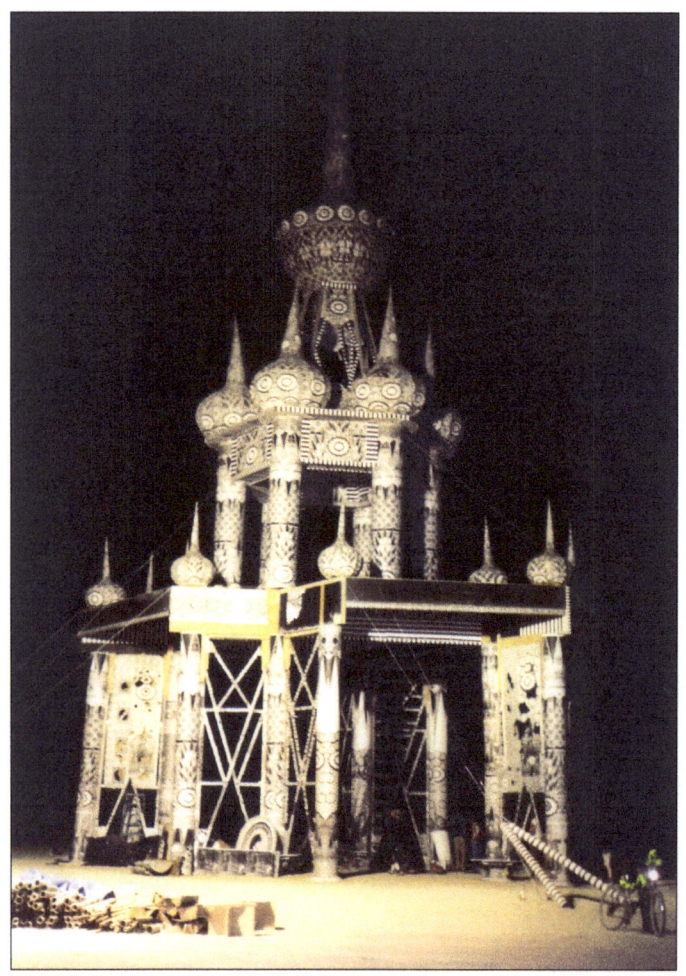

The Temple at the Burning Man Festival, 2003

The constant threat of police shutdown that permeated Utopian-style functions in New York City inspired me to travel to festivals in remote locations around the country such as Burning Man and the Rainbow Gathering in order to partake in fully immersive, transformative experiences. Every year, thousands of people voyage from points across the globe to participate in the creation of these ephemeral art-filled cities that thrive on radical self-expression, community spirit, and love. The influence of the Burning Man subculture has been especially far-reaching. The annual festival has sparked a boom of interest in avant-garde circus, belly dance, and fire arts, as well as a slew of offshoot interactive, costumed theme events and festivals that people attend in droves as they are continually encouraged to build the bridge between the worlds.

A week before my first trip to Burning Man in August 2003, I experienced a brief glimpse of a utopian society during one of the largest blackouts in New York City's history. For an entire day the machines lost power, and liminality prevailed. Liminality (from the Latin word limen, meaning "a threshold") is a shared trait amongst Utopian events that signifies an ephemeral quality of time marked by the reversal of hierarchies and suspension of sanctioned social norms.[16] During the blackout, New York City's mode of non-stop business-as-usual came to a grinding halt. The lights went out, and the air conditioners, subways, televisions and computers also lost power. Schedules and social programming gave way to a more relaxed sense of community. On this sticky summer night, many New Yorkers lounged outside their homes with their neighbors, partied on rooftops, and caroused in the streets. Corner stores graciously dispensed all of their ice cream and other perishable treats. People flocked in droves to the waterfront to picnic and watch the sun set. As the sun dipped behind the dark unlit silhouette of the Manhattan skyline a young man stood up and boldly proclaimed: "The city that never sleeps, sleeps!"

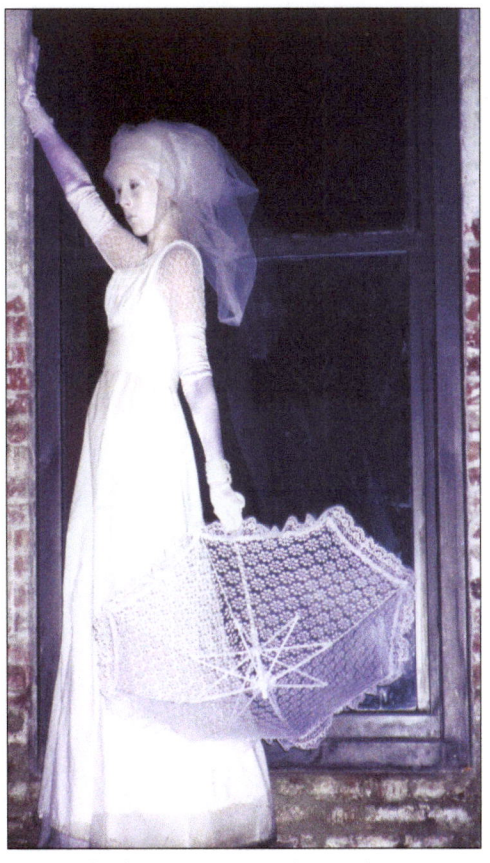

Performance art at a Lunatarium
warehouse party, NYC, 2002

But sleep it did not. Later that night the streets were swarmed with people curiously roaming in the dark. I followed the echoes of zealous clanging, back to the Grand Street waterfront where a renegade marching band had unleashed a cacophony of boisterous live music. Those who didn't have instruments picked up pieces of metal and wood, making music with whatever available implement they could find. The band down by the water evolved into a parade of a hundred or so revelers singing, dancing, and clanging in the pitch-black Brooklyn byways. And for a night, the streets of New York were ours.

---

16 *Liminality: occurs during intervals in the normally structured state of society…A betwixt and between threshold period. No longer do power and privilege, status and role, law and institution determine social inter-relatedness. (Rubenstien, 1992: 250)*

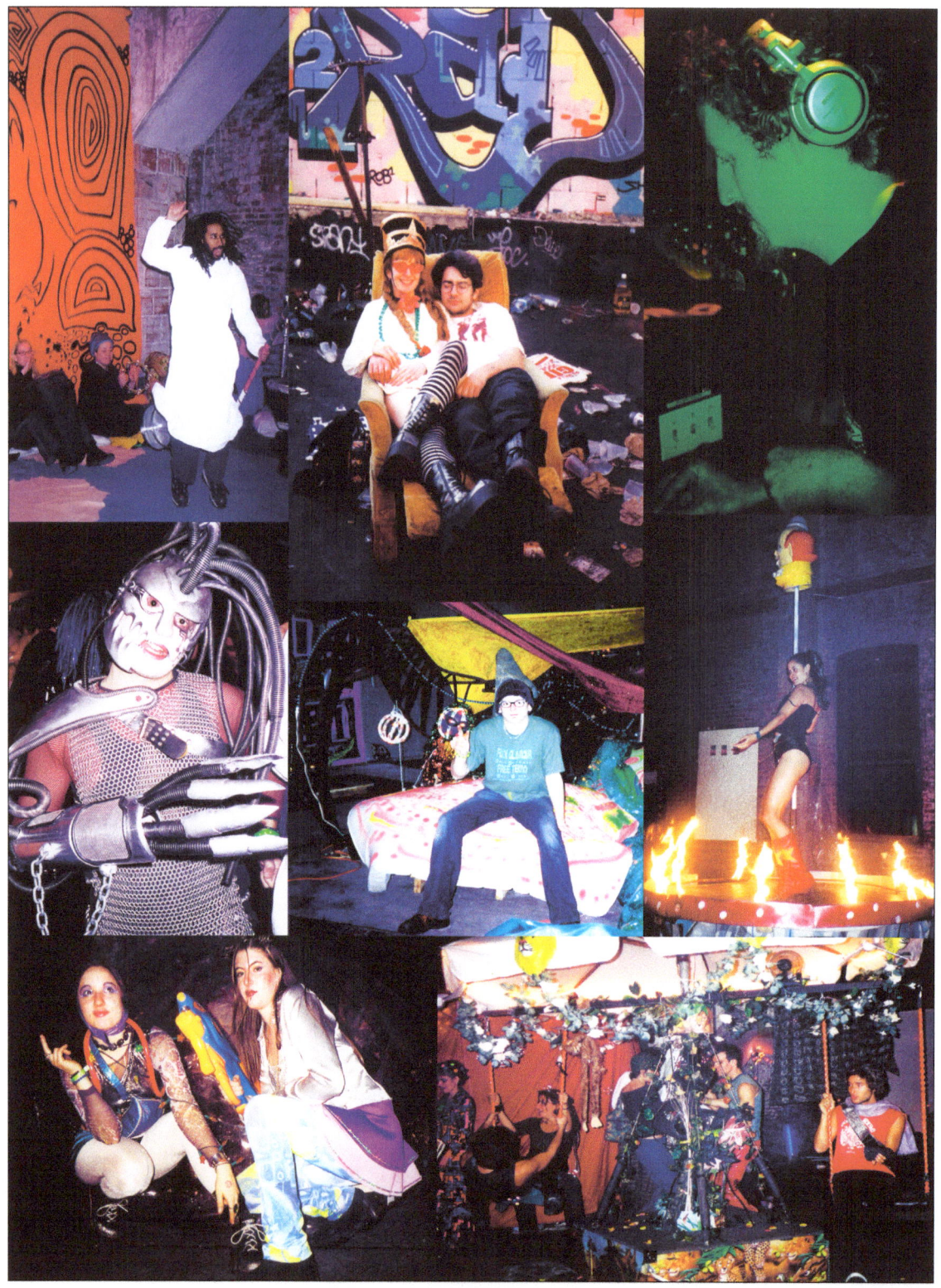

Brooklyn warehouse parties, 2002

WAREHOUSE PARTIES
NEW YORK CITY – 2001-2008

For many decades, New York City was hailed as an infamous international nightlife mecca and hallowed incubator of groundbreaking arts culture. Dance lovers, glitterati, and socialites from far and wide congregated nightly to partake in the gritty glamour of Manhattan's notorious nightclubs: Limelight, Tunnel, CBGB's, Paradise Garage, and Studio 54. Many artists who emerged from the platform of New York's underground club scene in the 1980s went on to achieve worldwide acclaim, including the Beastie Boys, Blondie, Basquiat, and Madonna. In the 1990s Mayor Rudolph Giuliani launched a "Quality of Life" campaign that resurrected the 1920s Prohibition-era Cabaret Laws and implemented sweeping re-zoning; paving the way for luxury developments that obliterated many of New York City's legendary nightclubs. Luxury condos, posh college dorms, shopping malls and chain restaurants sprouted up in their place. The majority of nightclubs that remain are highly regulated businesses with expensive cover charges; drink minimums, bottle service, aggressive security, and bureaucratic policies governing performance and art installations. As the avant-garde odyssey of Manhattan nightclubs became a distant glitter-soaked memory, underground culture migrated to the outer boroughs, with vibrant multi-media art parties being staged in post-industrial warehouses.

Warehouse parties became the next frontier in the creation of dynamic alternative subcultures in New York City in the post 9/11-era. These outrageous late-night spectacles fostered unprecedented diversity; attracting a cross-generational array of ravers, rockers, club kids, art stars, fetishists, Burning Man enthusiasts, and goths. Unconstrained by the confines of corporate sponsorships or mandates, warehouse parties became a vital channel for disseminating independent media while facilitating surreal and collaborative experiences in large unbridled spaces. Prominent venues for some of the most epic warehouse parties in N.Y.C included the Lunatarium, 38/9 Studios, and Rubulad, New York's longest running underground party that originated in the

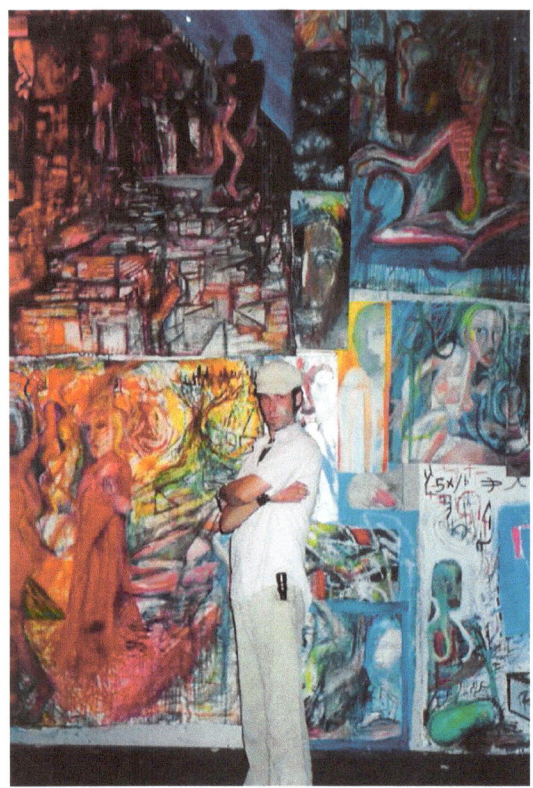

Visual art installation at the Lunatarium, 2002

> **IN TIMES OF REMEMBRANCE, OF CEASE-LESS TRANSFORMATION, WE SALUTE THE COURAGE AND RESILIENCE OF THIS BEAUTIFUL DIVERSE CITY. OVER THE PAST YEAR, WE AT LUNATARIUM HAVE WORKED DILIGENTLY TO BRING YOU A MULTITUDE OF EVENTS REFLECTING THE MANY COLORS, SENTIMENTS, AND EXPRESSIONS OF THIS CULTURAL MECCA. WE HARBOR A DEEP BELIEF IN THE ARTS AS A TOOL FOR HEALING, EDUCATION, AND LIBERATION. WITH YOUR HELP, WE HAVE STIRRED NEW VITALITY IN NEW YORK CITY AND PROVIDED A HOME FOR ARTISTIC VISIONARIES AND MUSIC LOVERS OF ALL KINDS. NEVER HAS IT BEEN SO CHALLENGING AND SO IMPORTANT.**

— **MESSAGE FROM THE LUNATARIUM CREW**
SEPTEMBER 11, 2002

late 1990s on the south side of Williamsburg, Brooklyn. Many events also took place at more obscure locations, where elaborate art-encrusted worlds were erected for the pleasure of just one night.

My introduction to New York's underground warehouse party scene occurred in October 2001 while working on a photojournalism assignment for a Costumes and Adornment documentary. After wrapping up a colorful interview on the topic of self-expression through modes of dress, one of my fur-and-glitter-clad subjects invited me to the Blackkat Halloween party at the Lunatarium. We trekked out to then-desolate DUMBO, Brooklyn and walked down Jay Street to a building along the water's edge, across from a sprawling power plant. We ventured inside and were escorted into an intergalactic freight elevator decked out with metallic foil, blue lights, ambient music, and a space alien operator. When we arrived at the top floor, the doors of the mother ship opened to reveal a cavernous 20,000 square foot warehouse that had been transformed into a realm beyond my wildest imagination: sexy superheroes, circus girls suspended from silks, star-spangled space cowboys, thrilling flame-throwing fire performances, dark circus carnival rides, tropical rainforest bathrooms, inflatable domes, screens with Technicolor video art, and revelers gyrating to the deep vibrating bass of techno music through the wee hours of the morning until the majestic sunrise.

As the sun rose over the city, light flooded in through the towering industrial warehouse windows and bathed everyone present. I found myself blissfully tearing up the dance floor with the music director of the Lunatarium, Rhiannon Erbach. In between stomps and twirls she turned to me and said: "The best time of the

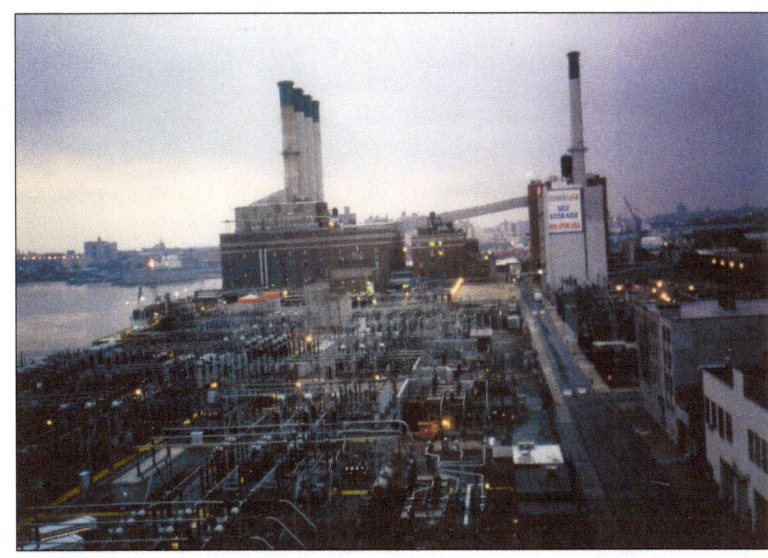

Sunrise view from a Lunatarium window, overlooking a Brooklyn power plant

party is being on the dance-floor at sunrise. By then people have sweat everything out and are reduced to their bare essence." And this was the moment we all lived for. It was this purity, pleasure, and transcendence that inspired so many individuals to participate in conjuring the ephemeral alternate reality in which these events would take place.

Collaborative by nature, warehouse parties require a resourceful team to procure décor, build art installations, barter with local businesses, book artists and manage the stages where a variety of independent bands, DJs, filmmakers, fashion designers, dance troupes, aerialists, fire performers, and visual artists are showcased. Amidst the din-and-clatter of the urban grind, warehouse parties cultivate an empowering arena for visionary minds to share upcoming art forms, cultivate their own rituals, and experience release from the pressures and confines of daily life.

In the years following 9/11, the NYPD vehemently targeted warehouse parties as if their mere existence was aiding and abetting terrorism. In 2003 an ominous law titled the Illicit Drug Anti-Proliferation Act (formerly known as the RAVE Act) was passed, increasing the government's authoritarian control over grassroots subcultures. This controversial legislation (Reduce America's Vulnerability to Ecstasy Act R. 2633) was initially vetoed by the senate after a large public outcry over the bill's violation of the First Amendment of the Constitution. The bill was renamed and surreptitiously added to an unrelated child protection bill (the AMBER Alert Act) without a public hearing, debate, or vote in Congress (Doig, 2003). Targeting nightlife and dance culture, the Illicit Drug

Anti-Proliferation Act authorized the federal government to dispense harsh fines and up to twenty years of jail time for venue owners and event producers that failed to thwart illicit drug use at an event, regardless of legitimate prevention efforts.

Another oppressive jurisdiction heavily enforced post-9/11 was the New York City Cabaret Laws. The prohibition-era cabaret laws were originally enacted in 1926 to curtail the impact of the thriving Harlem Renaissance jazz culture. Dancing was outlawed in all bars, clubs, and restaurants that did not possess a state-sanctioned license. In 1961, decades prior to Mayor Rudy Giuliani's quality of life campaign, more than 12,000 venues in New York City permitted dancing. By the end of 2002, the number had dwindled to less than 300 venues where people could legally dance (Romano, 2002).

In order to combat further cultural malaise, a coalition of nightlife activists formed the Metropolis in Motion organization to mobilize the fight against the cabaret laws. In May 2007, they co-produced the first ever "Dance Parade," which featured thousands of enthusiastic participants shimmying, gyrating, and twirling down 5th Avenue, representing more than 40 different styles of dance. This cherished pastime holds a special place in the heart of many New Yorkers, for whom dance is an artform integral to their lifestyle: a healthy physical release of stress, an instinctive form of communication, a reflection of heritage, a spiritual practice and a vehicle for transcendence. Dance Parade sought to cultivate a positive

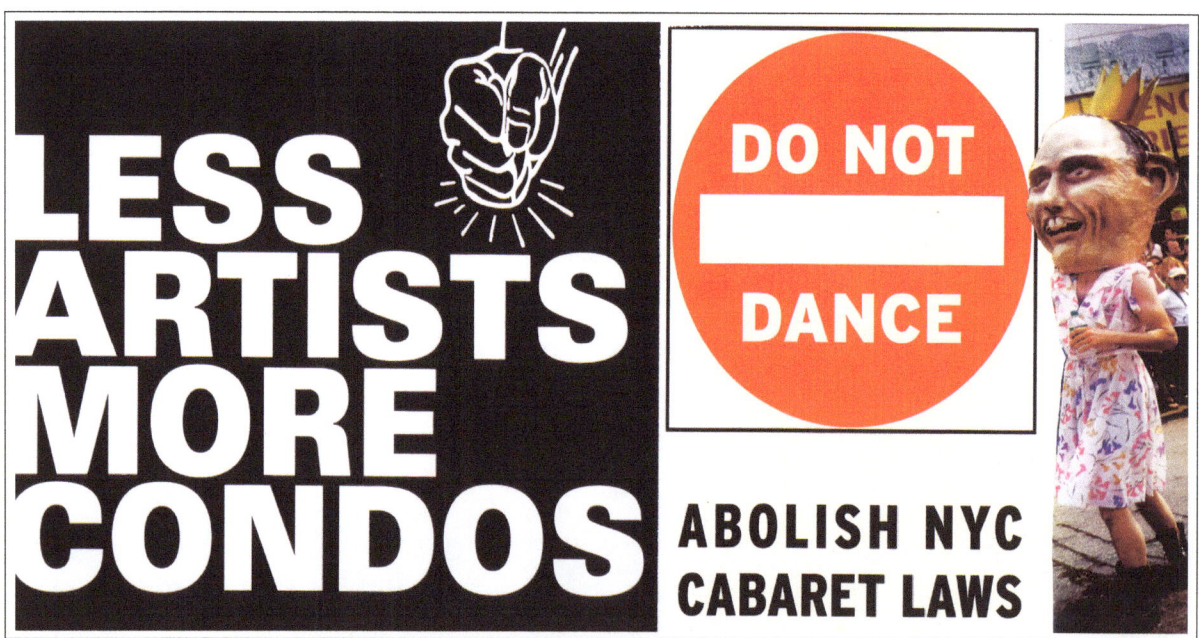

Mayor Giuliani's "Quality of Life" campaign

66

dialogue surrounding dance culture, highlighting its beauty and rich cultural legacy in order to gain momentum in the fight to overturn the NYC Cabaret Laws.

At the dawn of 2008 with nightlife and dance culture increasingly under fire, the NYPD raided three out of four of the large-scale warehouse parties ringing in the New Year. The first bust of the night was at a time-travel themed party in a remote section of Queens. The spacious industrial building that housed the festivities was brimming with colorful art installations, musicians, circus performers, and costumed revelers. Moments before the clock struck midnight, a dark cloud of police officers stormed into the party, turned on the lights, and shut off the music. They demanded that everyone exit the building and proceeded to arrest the event's organizers. It was a time travel-themed party indeed. Dressed to the nines as a scintillating flapper, I traveled back in time to the speakeasy days of the 1920s Prohibition, when gatherings were covert, alcohol was illicit, and jazz music was a scandal. Upon returning from my New Year's time travel debacle, I sadly acknowledged that not so much had changed.

The next stop on my New Year's misadventure was to the Rubulad party in Brooklyn, where I swam through a sea of wall-to-wall people and danced under a sky of sparkling stars, spaceships, colorful lights and disco balls. Shortly before 2 a.m., no fewer than a dozen police officers barged in to

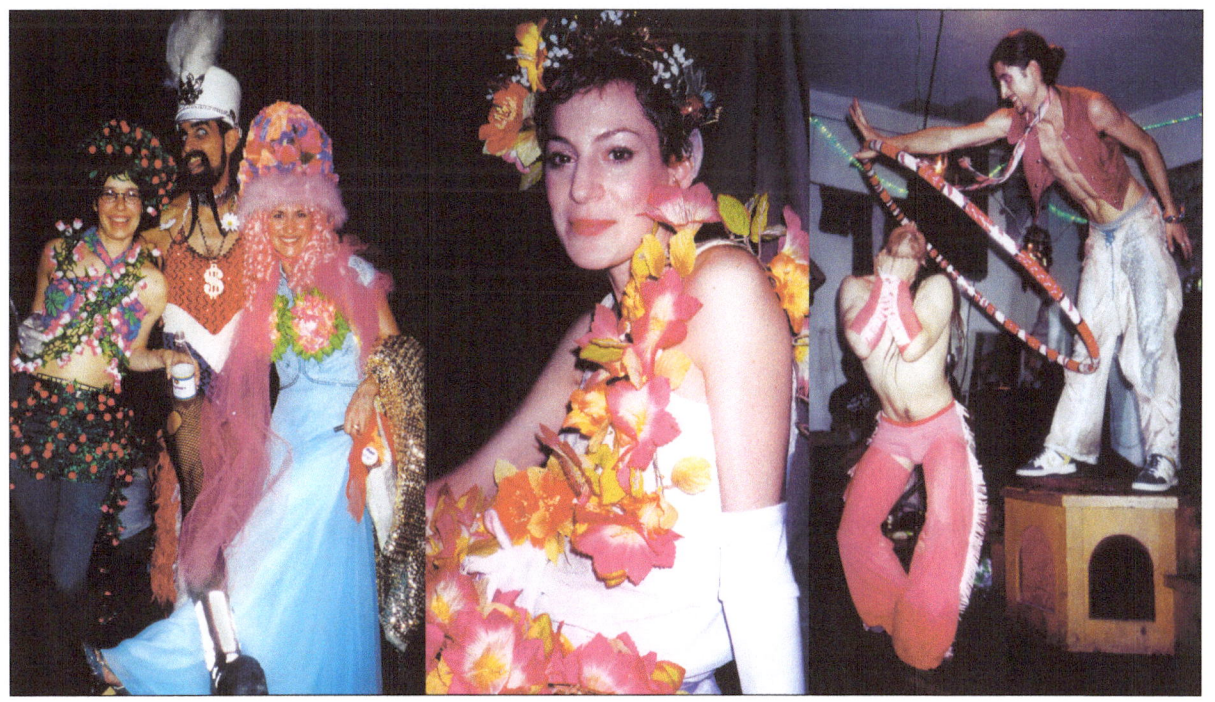

Costumed revelers at the Lunatarium and Rubulad warehouse parties, 2001-2003

shut the party down. It was beginning to feel like Groundhog's Day instead of New Year's. Once again, the police demanded that the DJ turn off the music and that everyone leave the building. But this time something much different transpired. While hundreds of disappointed partygoers quickly made for the exit, a couple hundred lingered indignantly inside.

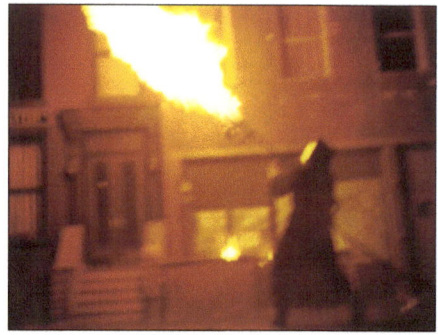

Fire show at 38/9 Studios, 2002

As the police attempted to finish emptying out the building, DJ Arrow Chrome got behind the turntables and turned the sound system back on. As the spirited beats pulsed from the speakers, DJ Chrome grabbed a microphone and made a gospel-like announcement to the crowd. "If you don't stand up, they're going to push you down! You gotta fight for your right to PARRRTY!" The remaining crowd whooped with jubilation, and quickly reclaimed their spots on the dance floor. And then, like a dream, the police were gone. Despite the officers firm demands that everyone go home, many defiant partygoers chose to stay and ring in the New Year, infused with the courage to stand up for their rights to gather and celebrate life. For one night, the people took on the system and won, dancing triumphantly into the sunrise.

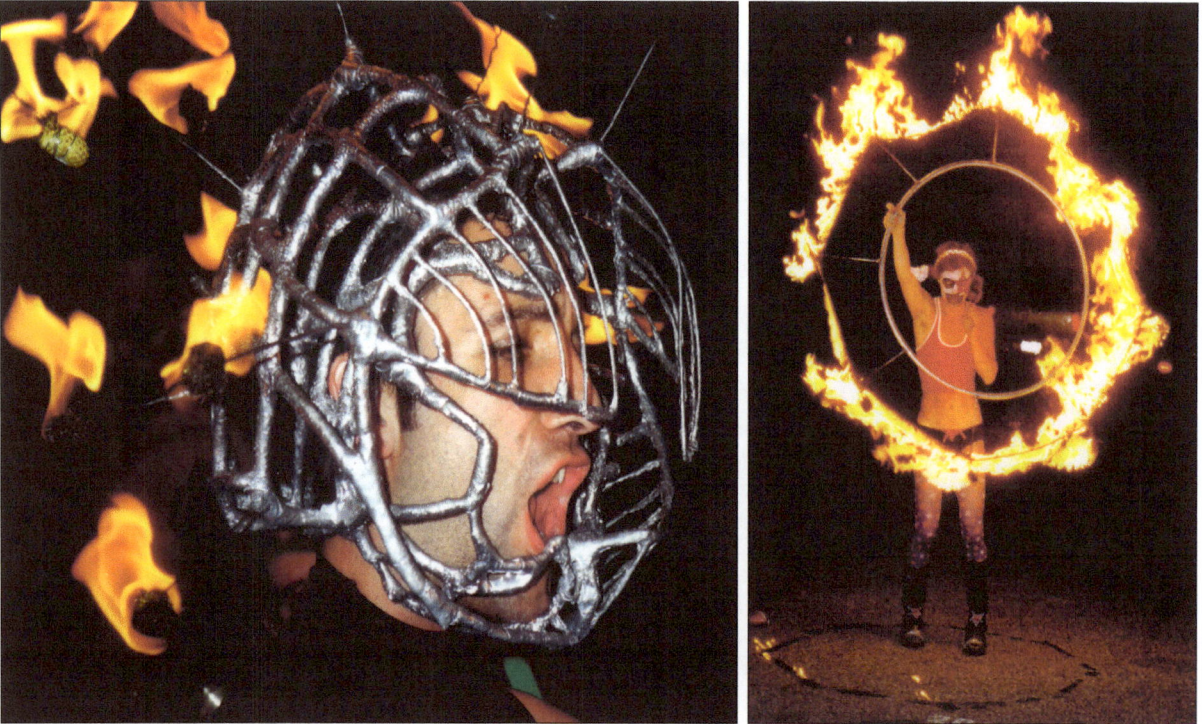

Flambeaux ritual fire performance, New York City, 2001

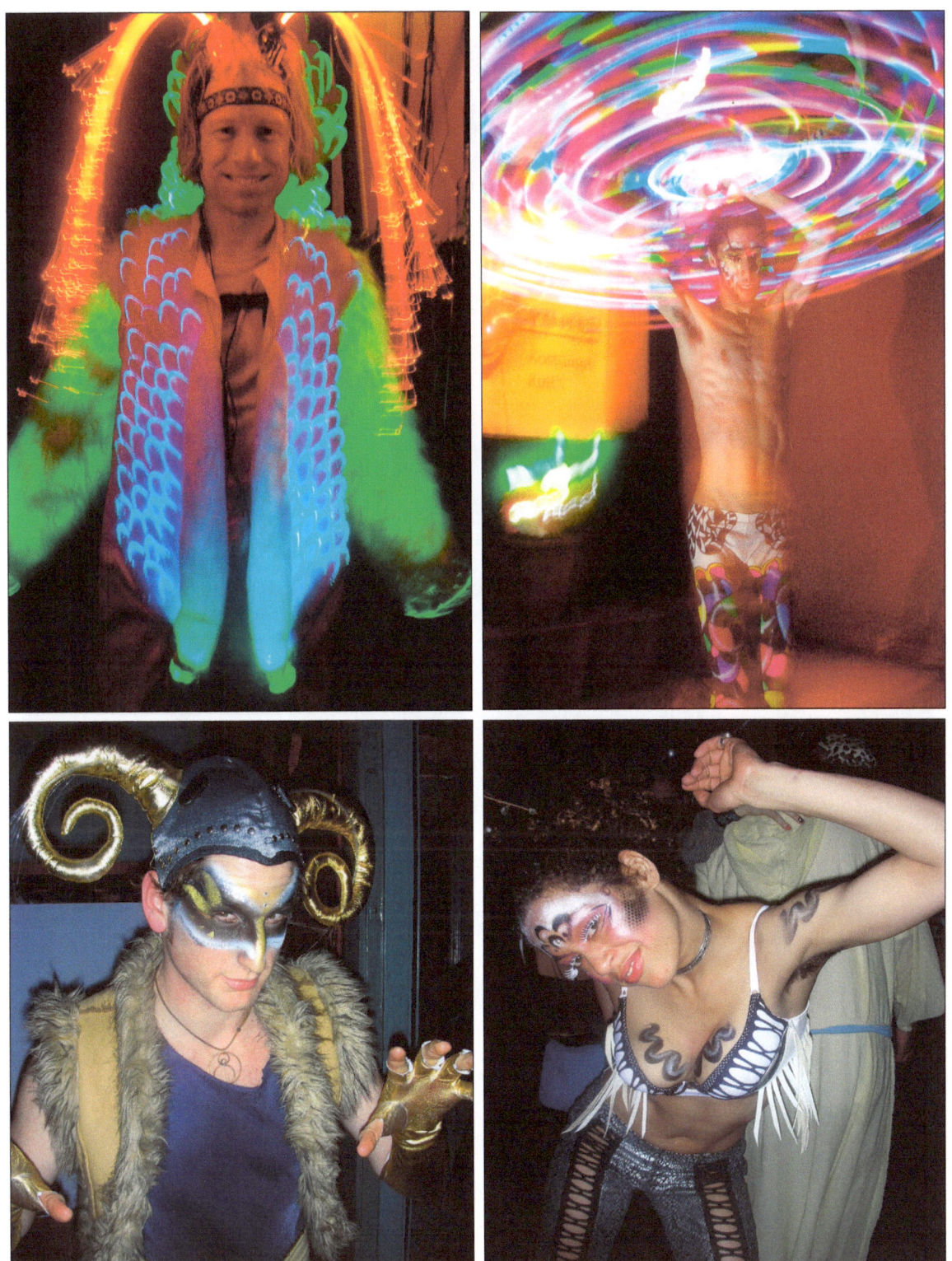

Kostume Kult Burning Man fundraiser party, NYC, 2007

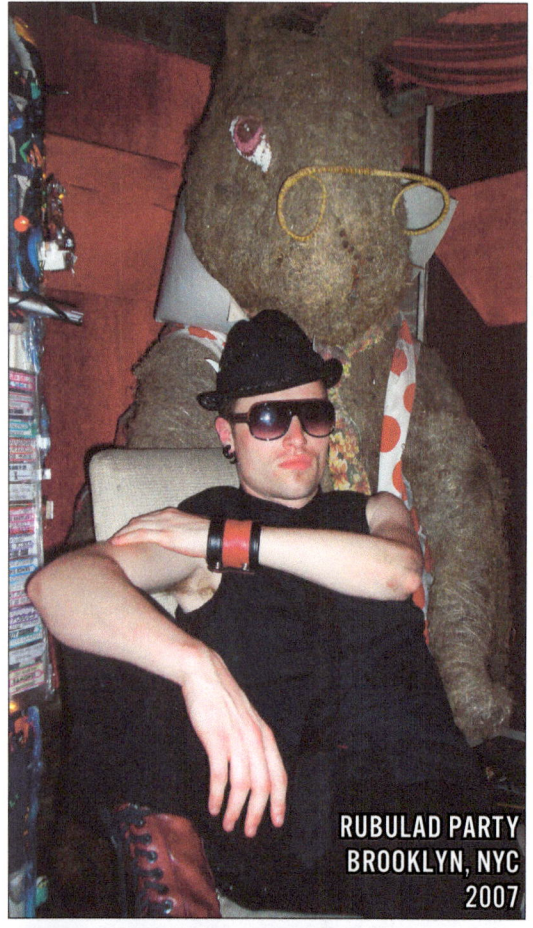

RUBULAD PARTY
BROOKLYN, NYC
2007

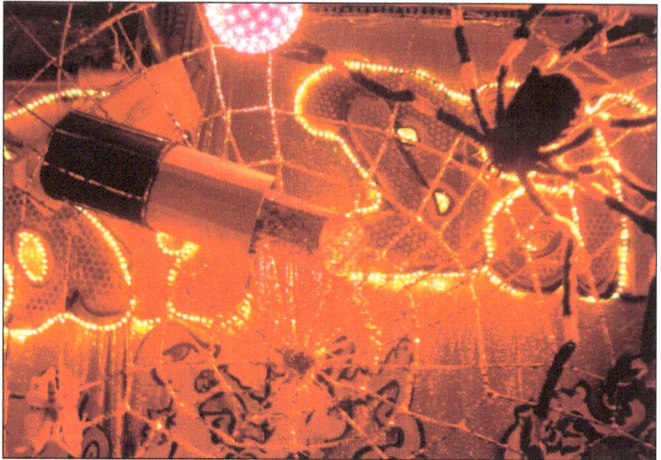

"Where else can you go out, not know anyone, dress up in costume, catch the subway, find a crazy party, dance like a maniac to bitchin' music, see a couple of awesome ska and dub bands, love being refreshingly drenched by the rainus humidious, swear obnoxiously in French, at French people but end up having an unlikely German conversation, get shot by a cap gun in the arse 3 times and beg for more, get busted by the cops (not again… whine), continuing partying in secret regardless, roll around having onstage sparkle-snow tongue wrestling with an anticipatory tantalizing fervor, and have your lily white hiney walloped with a leather strap in front of onlookers and loving it… and all within a few hours of stepping off the plane?"

– Rudi Yardley (left) of Melbourne, Australia

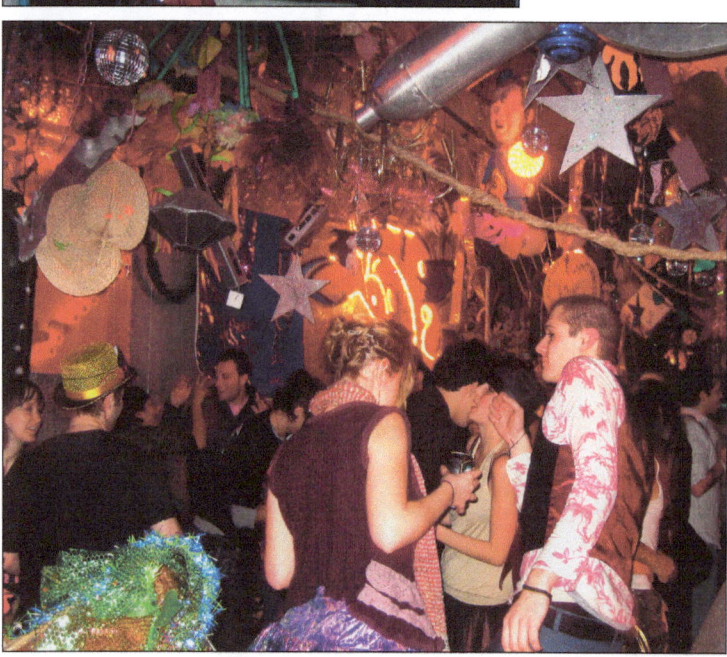

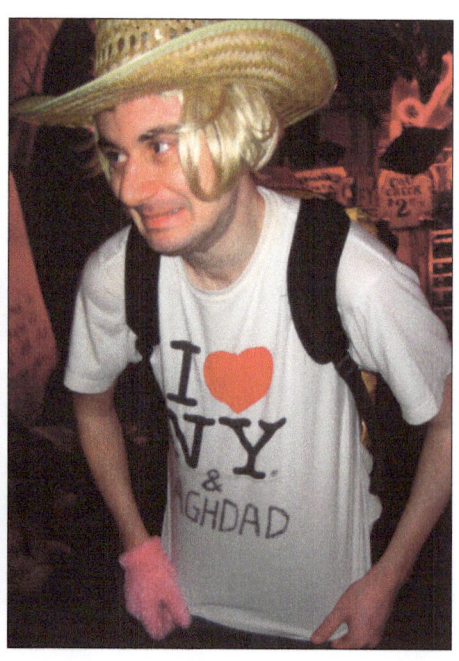

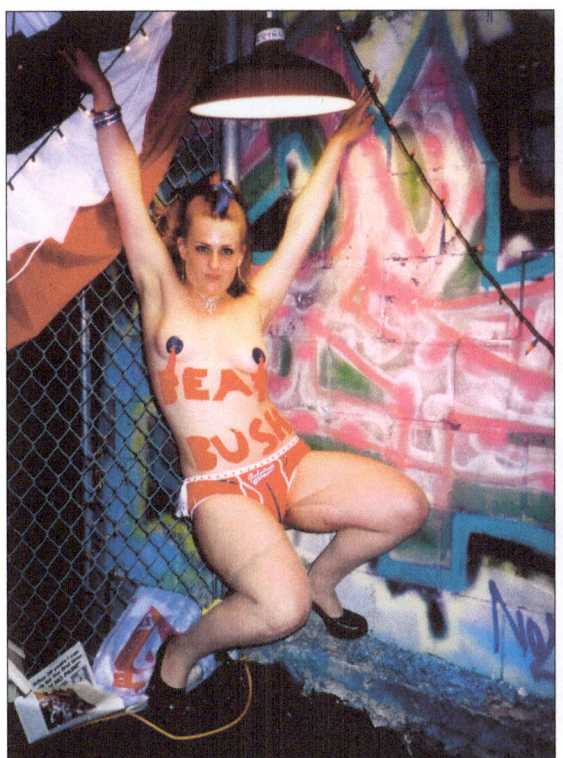

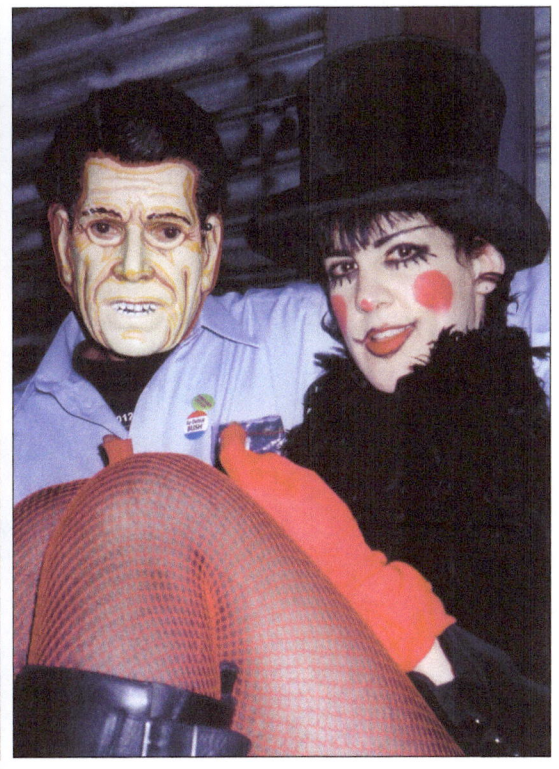

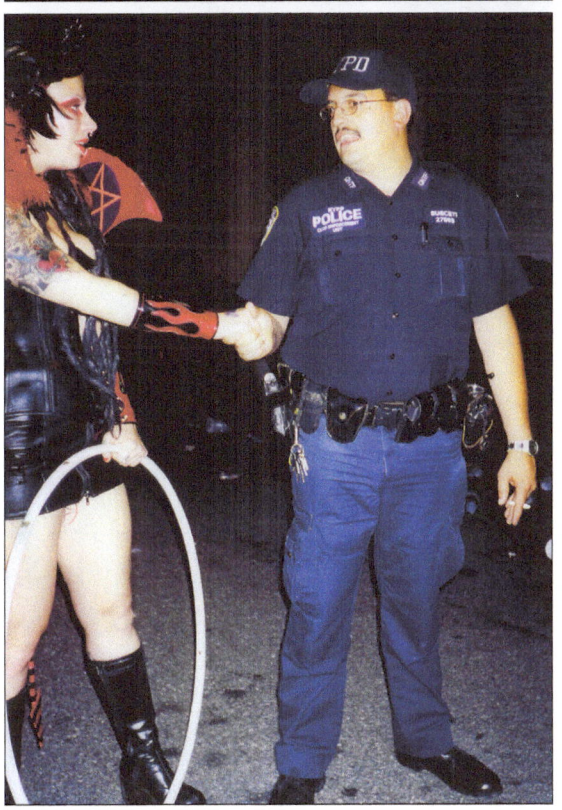

" **THANK YOU MR. OFFICER FOR NOT SHUTTING DOWN OUR PARTY...** "

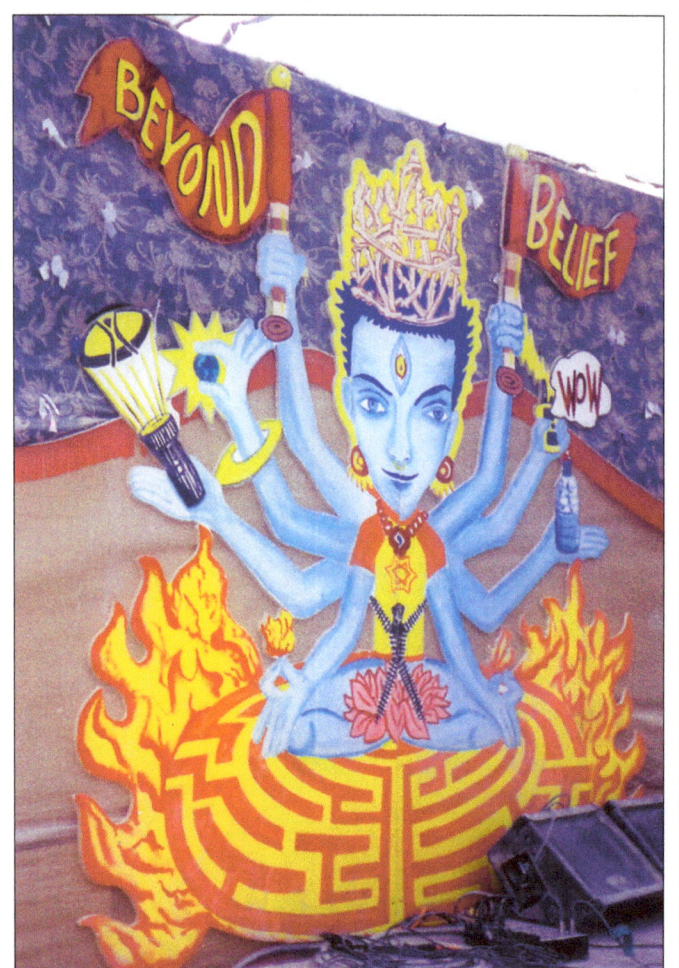
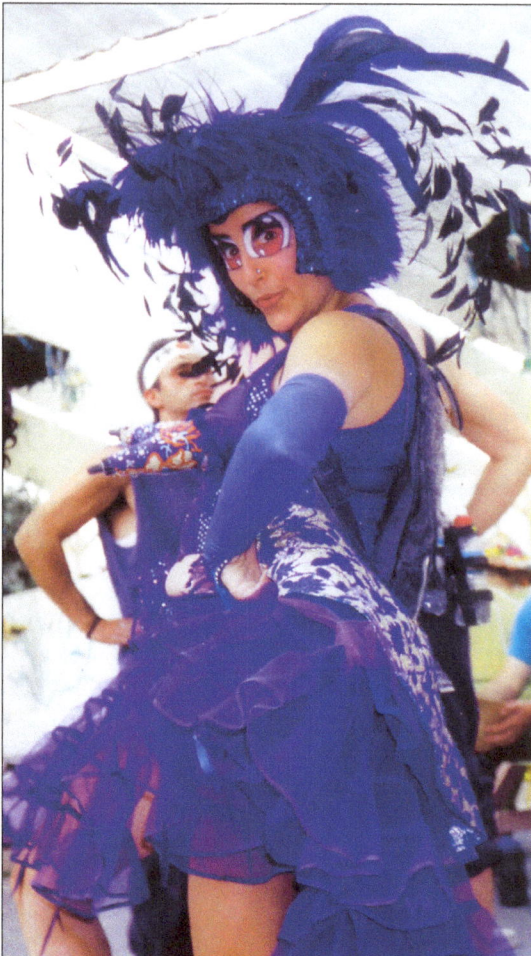
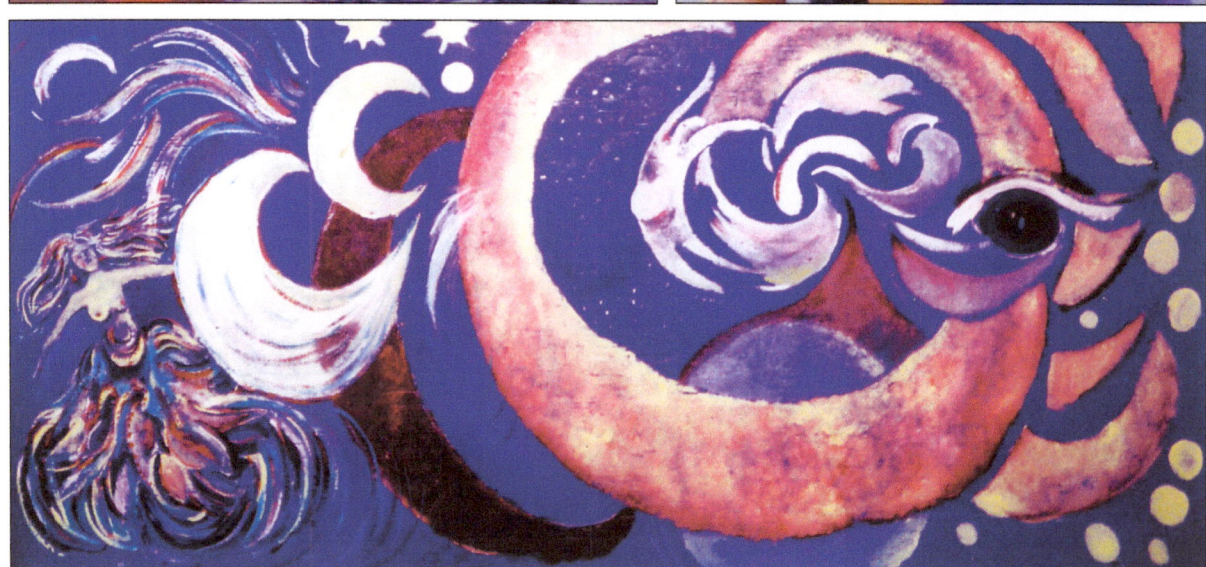

Center Camp at the Burning Man Festival, Black Rock City, Nevada, 2003

BURNING MAN
FESTIVAL – 2003

The first incarnation of the Burning Man festival took place in 1986 at Baker's Beach in San Francisco, California. During an intimate ritual with 20 participants, the festival's founder Larry Harvey burned an eight-foot tall wooden man in honor of the summer solstice. In 1990 Burning Man migrated to the Black Rock desert in Nevada (fondly coined "the playa"), after the San Francisco police banned the gathering from burning the effigy on the local beach. In the coming decades, Burning Man grew exponentially to become a dazzling annual extravaganza. On its tenth anniversary in 1996, over 8,000 thrill-seekers attended the still-obscure weeklong festival. By 2003, Burning Man had assumed the proportions of a small city, inhabited by 30,000 temporary residents (Burning Man, 2008). In 2011, Burning Man reached capacity with ticket sales of more than 50,000; for the first time ever the world-renowned event had sold out.

The San Francisco bay area is the spiritual birthplace of the Burning Man subculture, however over time the event has evolved to encompass an international artist community with people traveling from all over the world to attend the annual festival. Many loyal Burning Man enthusiasts participate in a plethora of year-round preparatory activities including logistical infrastructure planning meetings, fundraiser parties for theme camps, performance rehearsals, extensive production for elaborate art installations and costume workshops. Concurrent to its many community-oriented functions, the festival promotes "radical self-reliance" by offering minimal commerce in a rugged natural environment. The Black Rock desert hosts a world of extremes with sweltering hot days, frigid nights, storms with high winds, and the all-pervasive alkaline dust. Amidst a culture of radical self-reliance, the harsh living conditions on the playa foster a genuine camaraderie that inspires people to support each other's journey and survival.

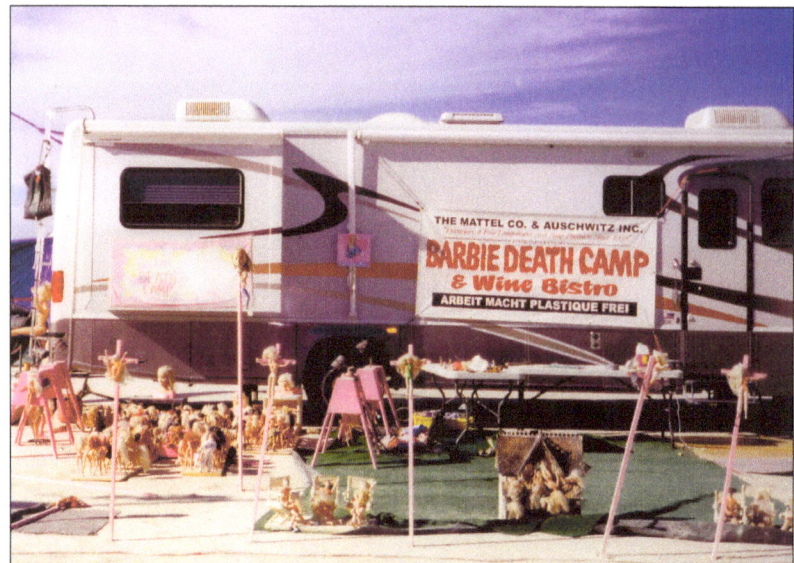

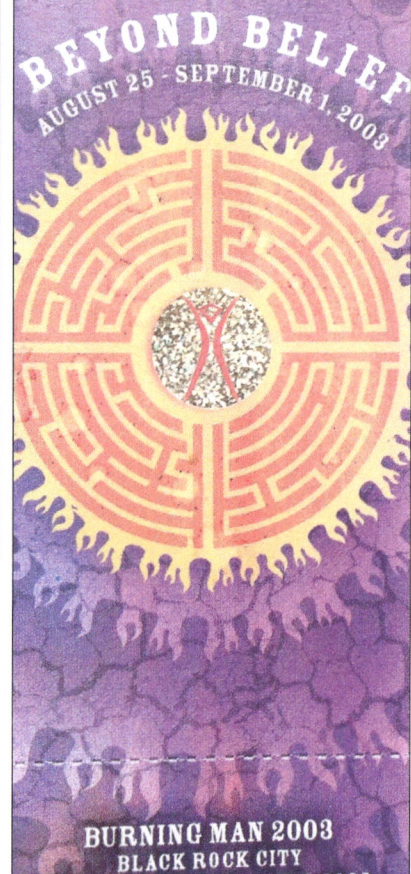

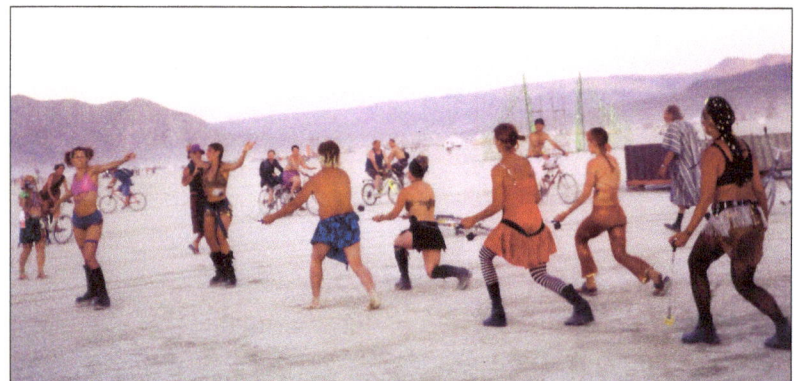

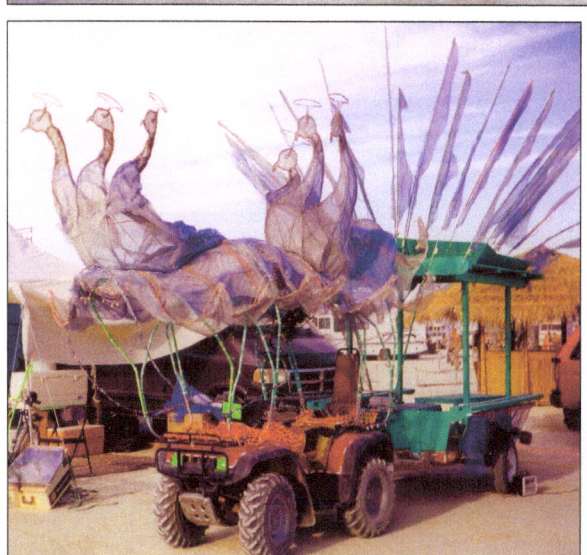

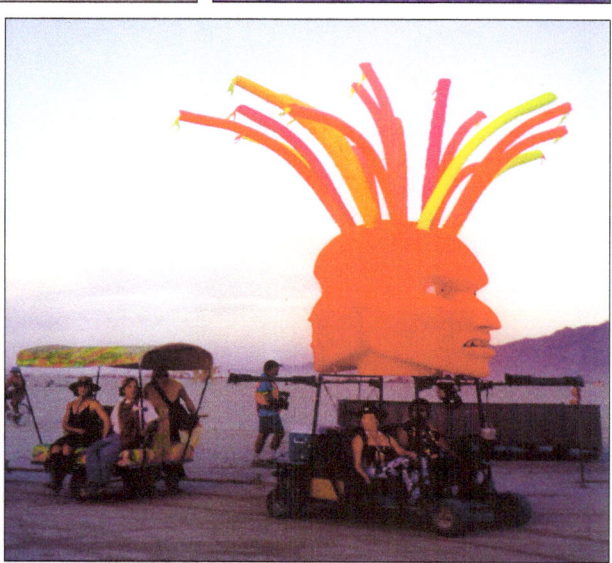

Parades, art cars, and theme camps, Burning Man Festival, 2003

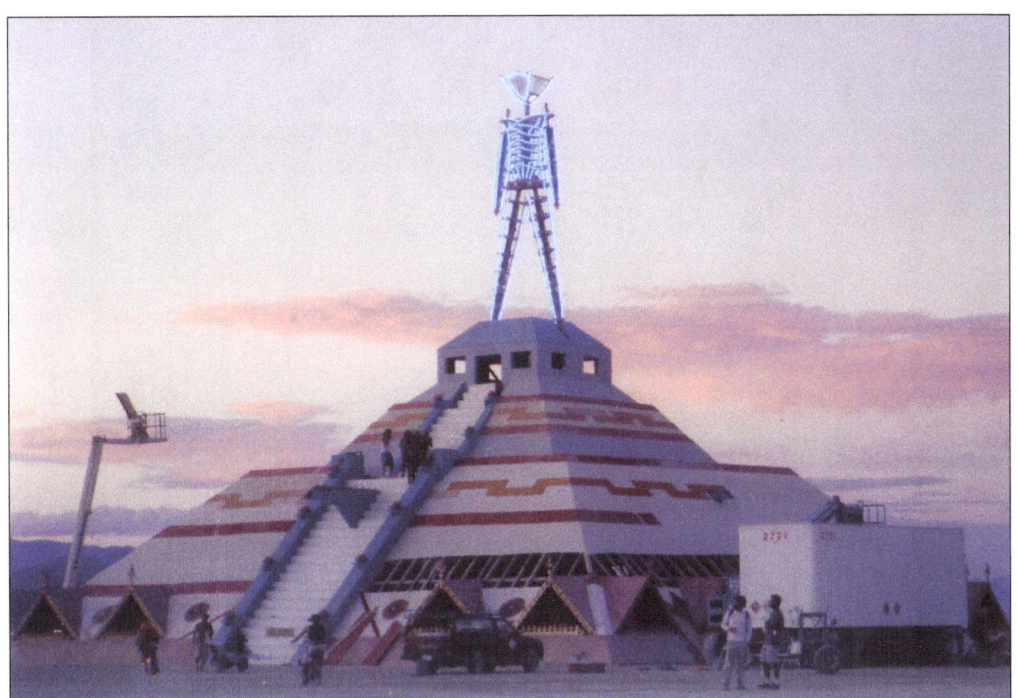

Work in progress: Construction of the Man, Burning Man Festival, 2003

During the last week in August thousands of party pilgrims embark on an odyssey into the barren Black Rock desert, voyaging from lands far and wide in search of bliss and catharsis. In 2003, I made this exhilarating journey for the first time. After flying across the country from New York to San Francisco, and then driving for eight hours into the sweltering desert my caravan arrived in Gerlach, Nevada. The desolate old west town with less than 200 residents is the last inhabited patch of civilization before arriving at Burning Man. Here, my party got out of the van to buy ice-cold beverages, stretch our legs, and use real bathrooms for one last time. We departed from Gerlach down a seemingly endless dusty road. "Riders on the Storm" by the Doors crackled faintly on the radio invoking the sensation of serendipity and excitement for the adventures that were to come.

Upon arrival at the gates of Burning Man, we were greeted by ticket-takers clad in tutus, cowboy hats, and combat boots. They thoroughly checked our vehicle for stowaways, gave heartfelt hugs, and offered a warm "welcome home." Next they inquired if there were any "virgins" among us. Burning Man first-timers are required to undergo the rite of passage rituals of ringing the virgin bell at the gate and assuming "playa names." These monikers mark an identity transformation away from the confines of daily life. Some of the festival's participants live flamboyant, artistic lifestyles year-round, but for many others Burning Man is a celebratory respite where they go to be whoever they want to be while immersed in a world of eclectic, provocative cavorting.

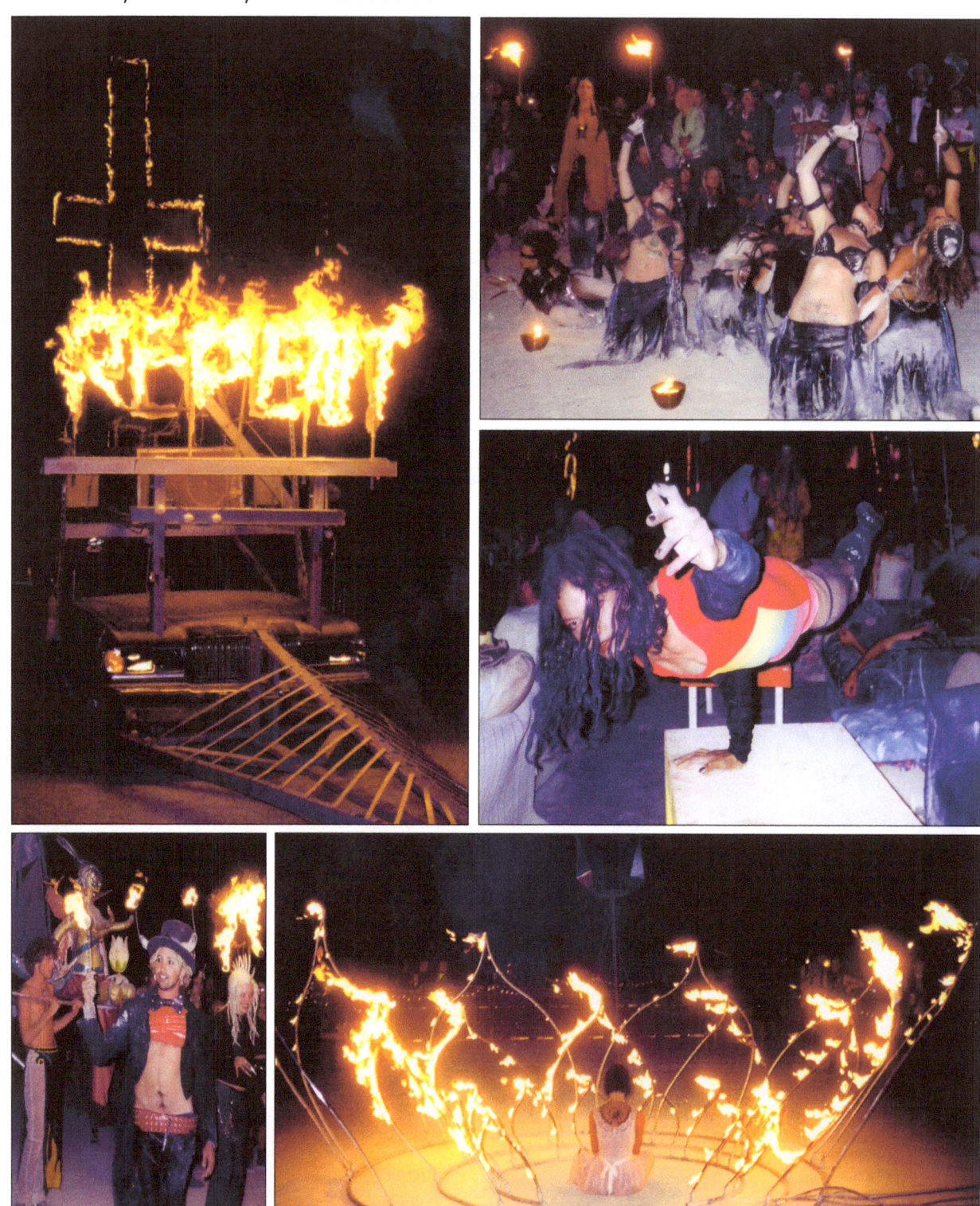

Fire rituals and circus arts, Burning Man Festival, 2003

Burning Man embodies a liminal society where participants experience the magic of a great city rising and falling within a week. My first day on the playa I witnessed the city grow before my eyes as I rode my bike out at sunset to watch the Man and Temple being built. From this point on, the rise and fall of the sun marked time; electronic communication and time-keeping devices were rendered obsolete. Within the confines of the festival, traditional hierarchy, privileges, and prohibitions are suspended. The mood is one of ecstasy and release, celebrating the temporary liberation from the bondage of normal protocol. Many cultures all over the world partake in annual liberation festivals including the Jewish holiday Purim, New Orleans Mardi Gras, and Brazilian Carnival. These celebrations share a core element

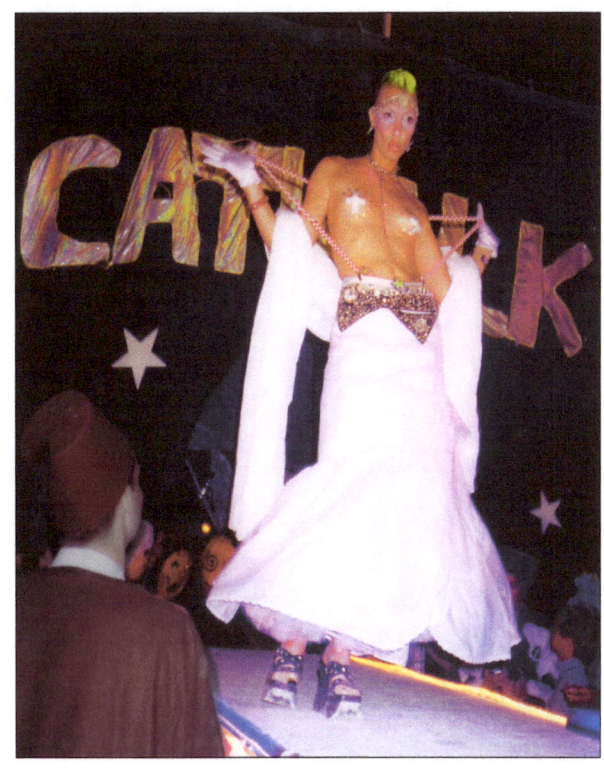

Catwalk fashion show, Burning Man Festival, 2003

with Burning Man: for a brief moment in time anything goes.[17] But when you look beyond the realm of decadent carousing that is synonymous with Burning Man, you see thousands of people defying passive consumer society by actively creating their own culture. This makes many aspects of the Burning Man festival an empowering alternative to the mainstream status quo.

At Burning Man, formalities that apply in everyday life are banished in exchange for a temporary city built upon the tenets of radical-self expression. My days at the festival were spent soaking in the sights of ornate costumes, hitching rides on mutant vehicle art cars, and exploring gargantuan art installations. I attended all-night dance parties, holistic workshops, open-mic cabarets, fashion shows and powerful ritualistic performances with chanting, dancing, drumming, and fire. In 2003, the scale of art and performances at Burning Man had reached mind-blowing proportions with more than 500 theme camps, a mobile half-scale 16th century pirate ship named La Contessa, a breathtaking 30 foot tall fallen chandelier

---

17   *Elaborate pageants, grotesque masks, drunken revelry, noise making, buffoonery, burning effigies, costume parades, feasts with special delicacies, and every manner of carousing and merrymaking ... On Purim "all things are permissible" (Rubenstein, 1992: 247).*

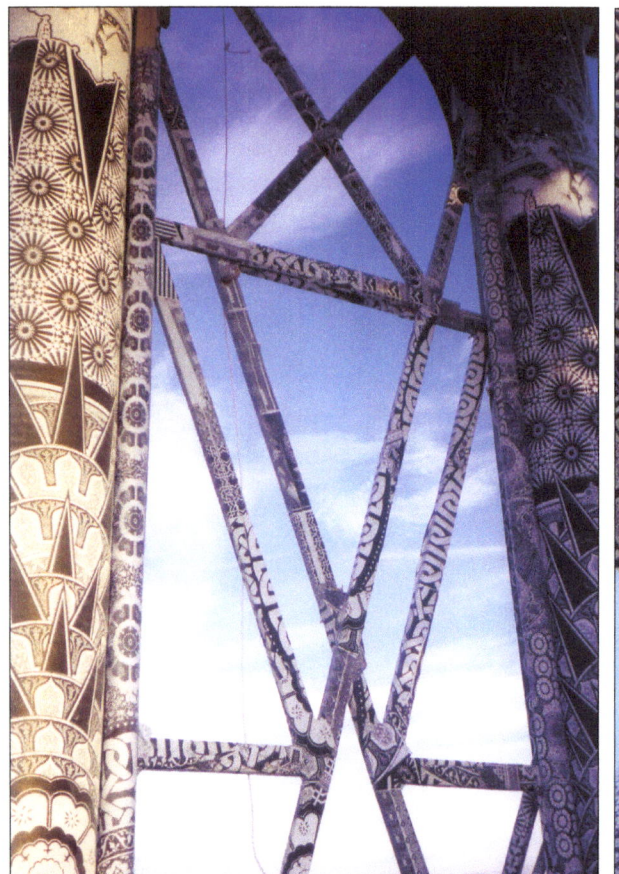
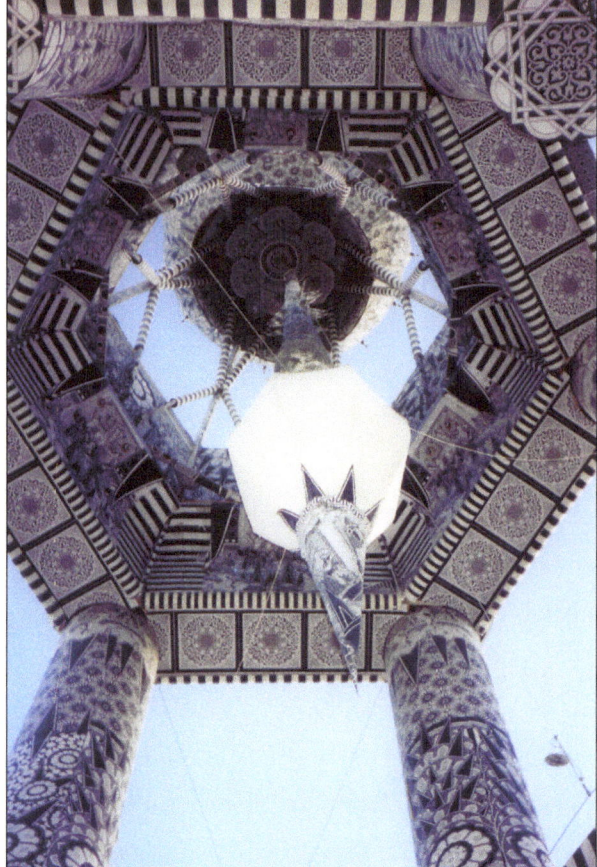
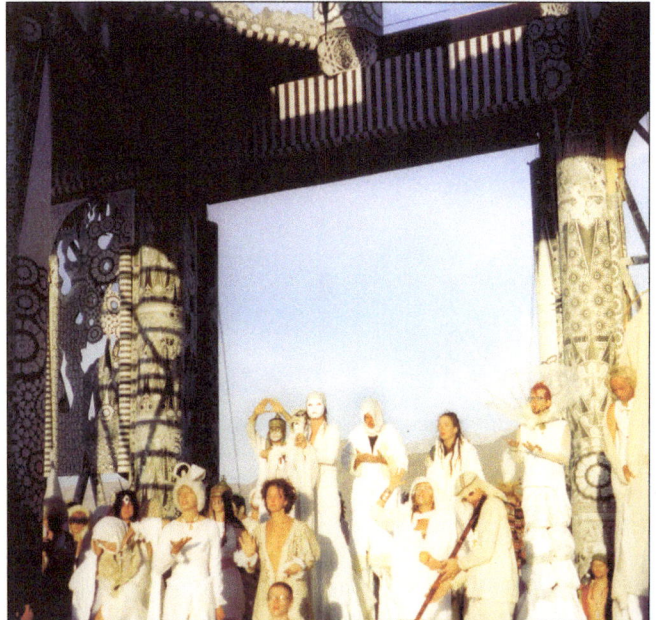
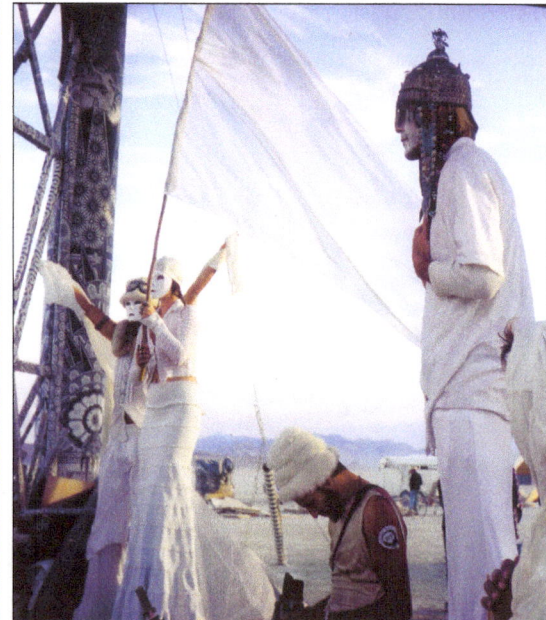

Sunrise ritual at the Temple, Burning Man Festival, 2003

sculpture out on the deep playa, the Gravity Installation with two-ton slabs of concrete suspended from a towering skeletal metal structure, a free, fully-stocked costume boutique courtesy of Kostume Kult, daring aerial feats by dark cabaret circus troupe Xeno, neo-tribal belly dance performances by Ultra Gypsy and a post-burn multimedia spectacular stage show by the Mutaytor.

Amidst the labyrinth of spectacle and curiosities that is Burning Man, the Temple is built to honor the more somber facets of life, where people can engage in ritual practice and pay respects to the dead. Unlike most places of worship where it would be considered vandalism, the Temple at Burning Man is a shared space of spiritual veneration on which people are encouraged to write and draw. Early one morning, after waking up on a trampoline and experiencing the most mind-blowing fireball sunrise, I road my bike out to the Temple to create an effigy for a deceased loved one, in hopes of shedding painful feelings I no longer wanted to carry. As I finished making my mark on the Temple, the most beautiful morning ritual procession entered; all in white, towering on stilts, wearing masks, and robes. The ritual performers embodied mystical spirits worshipping at the dawn of a new day. They gave out eggs, which symbolized life, wholeness, and the interconnectedness of all beings. The low, deep hum of the didgeridoo majestically silenced everyone present. The air was sultry and sweet with the smoke from burning sage. Many people were embracing and crying. I intuitively felt the sadness of the earth spirits, for the environment that is being destroyed by pollution and indigenous cultures that have been annihilated by genocide. On the final night of the festival the Temple is burned along with the effigies for lost loved ones, prayers, and emotional baggage.

At Burning Man 2003 there was also a church of a different sort, with headlining performances by Reverend Billy and the Church of Stop Shopping. Reverend Billy is an anti-consumerism performance artist evangelist, who brought his entire two dozen-person robe-clad choir from New York to Black Rock City to preach the doctrine of "replacing shopping with love." The Reverend's sermons were one of the few overtly political performances at Burning Man 2003 that correlated American consumerism with driving violent foreign policies. He emphasized that we are all guilty of rampant consumption, but are capable of reforming. Reverend Billy encourages retail and mass media interventions: "Put your hand on that product and pull it back. Enter the post-corporate reality. There's nothing like American consumerism, except for a crack cocaine addiction... Grass roots must reclaim the media. When the media monopoly increased from 25 to 35 percent it resulted in 805 losses of dependent producers. We must become the media!" Reverend Billy and the Church of Stop Shopping's enthusiastic performance had me singing for the rest of the trip. "Start stopping, you better stop shopping... We'll never shop again! Forever and Amen... Hallelujah Stop Shopping!"

PARADES, PARTIES, AND PROTESTS

In keeping with the theme of radical self-reliance at Burning Man, no commerce takes place on the festival grounds with the exception of ice and coffee sold at Center Camp. The overwhelming advertising and consumer choices that bombard people in their daily lives are temporarily replaced with equally overwhelming amounts of art, expansive desert terrain, and intense human interaction. For a brief and titillating moment in time, corporations lose their all-pervasive power. In 2003, the debunking of corporate dominion was celebrated in numerous art installations including the Barbie Death Camp & Wine Bistro, and the Costco Soul Mate Trading Outlet. Within the confines of the festival grounds, the economy at Burning Man is based on

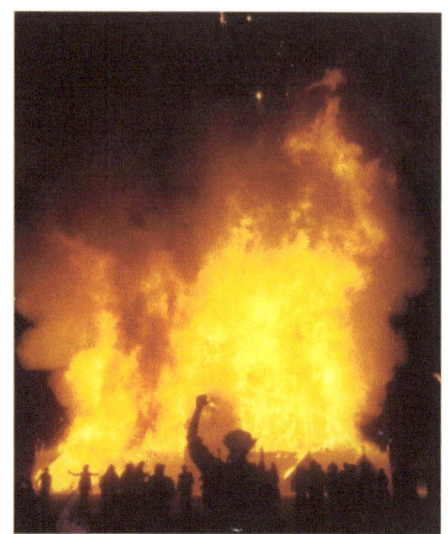

Burning the Man, 2003

barter and gift giving. This correlates with the Native American potlatch custom, in which abundance is shared throughout the community. That same year, the beautiful, scantily clad denizens of the Fuzzy Nation handed out hundreds of multicolored scarves at the festival to spread the joy of gift giving. Year round, members of the collective sold the scarves for $10 each, informing customers that buying one scarf would provide two other people with scarves as gifts. Towards the end of the week at Burning Man, the Fuzzy Nation hosted a fashion show to demonstrate the many different ways in which the scarves could be worn and to encourage its audience to embrace the gift economy and incorporate it into their daily lives.

After a week of enlightened debauchery, the official climax of this hallowed festival is the ritual burning of the Man. The energy on the playa was electric with anticipation by Saturday night as tens of thousands of costumed revelers and mutant vehicle art cars encircled the Man. The iconic structure was made of neon lights and latticed wood and stood at 32-feet tall, perched firmly atop a 47-foot tall art-deco pyramid. Hundreds of fire dancers performed in the annual pre-burn conclave ritual around the Man's base with a thrilling array of fire fans, flaming hoops, spinning poi, and burning staffs. At the conclusion of the performance, his arms were raised along with the mounting anticipation of the massive crowd. I watched wide-eyed as breathtaking fireworks were launched from the inside of the towering wooden structure, shooting glittering trails hundreds of feet into the air. The crowd erupted ecstatically as the Man was engulfed with flames, and went completely wild when he began to crumble. Sparks and burning embers were violently propelled by a mini dust devil. Revelers dodged the flaming particles while shrieking with fear and delight. Once the most intense part of the burn subsided, the crowd ran toward the burning wreckage leaping and twisting over the pyre, rejoicing in primal urges of the spirit being nourished.

Burning Man is part potlatch, ritual, art festival, and survival test. After a week of unusually sublime weather, I had begun to take the survival element for granted. On the last day of the event, I went to fly a kite at the far end of the playa with friends from my camp. Without warning the sun was eclipsed by an opaque white swarm, and a blinding blanket of dust propelled by thrashing winds overcame us. In the eye of the storm, I could see no more than a few inches in front of me. I crouched down to the ground and put my arms over my face, while gasping for air and waited for the whiteout to pass. With no shelter to protect me, I felt naked and vulnerable at the mercy of nature while fully immersed in the raging elements. It was humbling to be confronted with my own mortality and an awareness of nature's power as the divine giver and taker of life. The experience renewed my intentions to have utmost respect for the natural world, to appreciate my health, and not take life for granted.

By the last day of Burning Man there are few land markers left. Camps are torn down and hauled away in crates or consumed by fire. Burning bins filled with the remains of effigies and art installations are set ablaze all across the playa. The week's spell is broken. The city quickly becomes a shell of itself as departing revelers are encouraged to "leave no trace." Following the arduous mass exodus, the dedicated members of the Black Rock City Department of Public Works stay on the playa for several weeks to break down the physical infrastructure of the event and rid the land of any remaining party particles. In order for the Burning Man festival to continue and for permits to be re-issued, the entire city must disappear. Ashes to ashes, dust to dust… and not a speck of glitter remains.

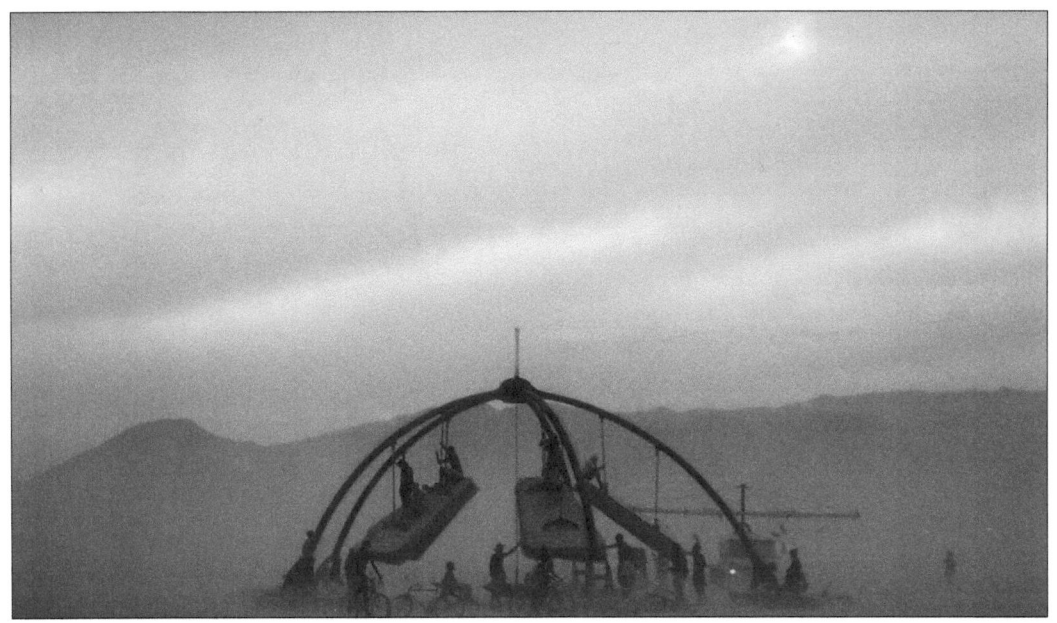

Gravity Installation post-dust storm, Burning Man Festival, 2003

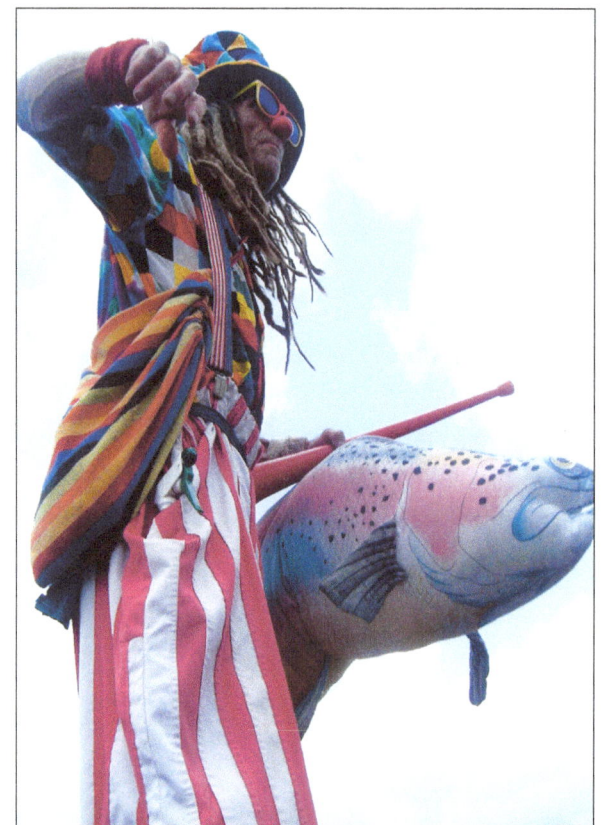
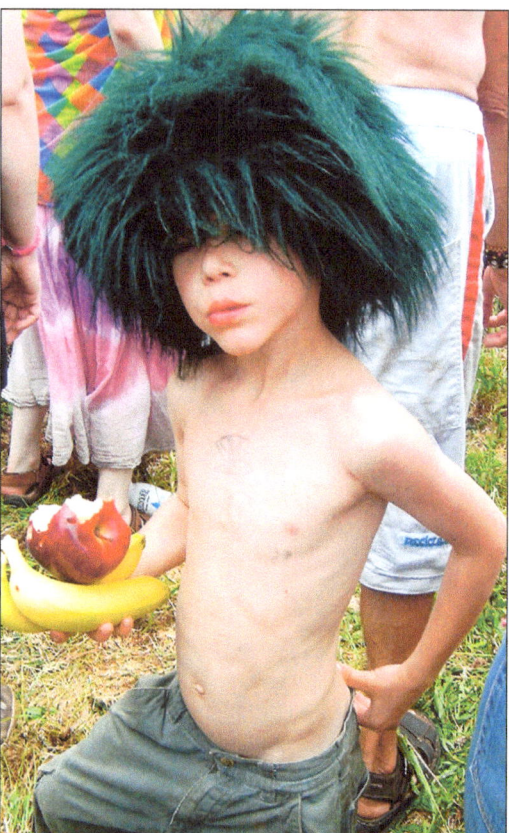
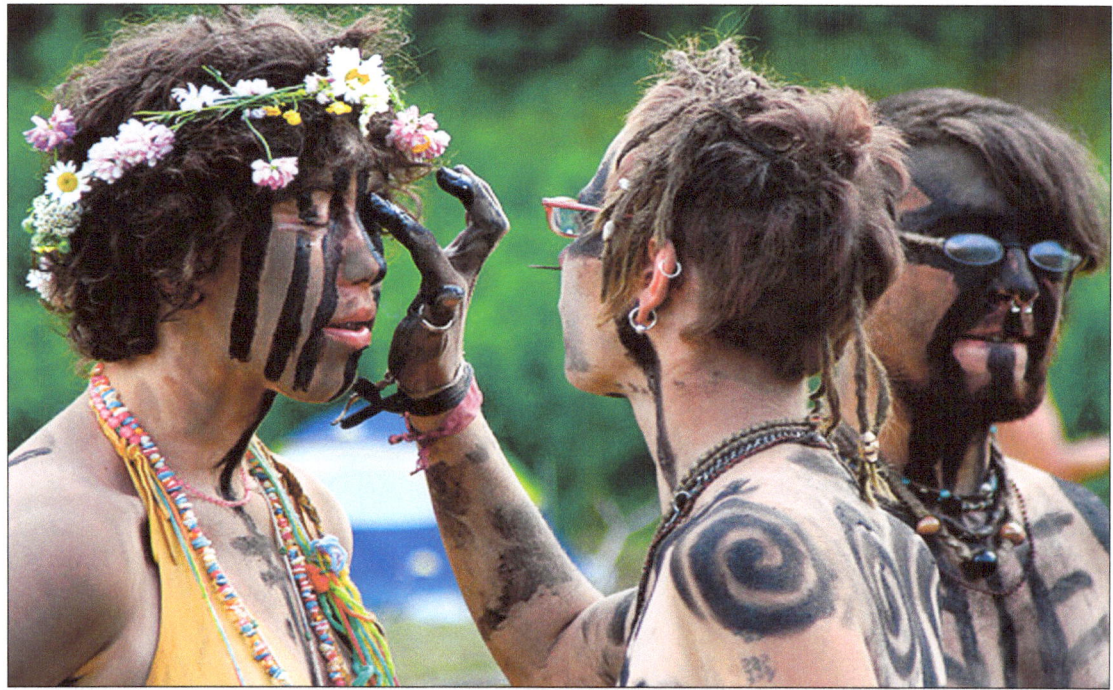

Radical self-expression at the Rainbow Gathering, West Virginia, 2005

RAINBOW GATHERING – 2005

The first official Rainbow Gathering took place in July 1972, deep in the forest of the sacred Table Mountains in Colorado. The four-day long celebration culminated on July 4th with thousands of people engaged in a silent meditation ritual for world peace. One of the focal points of the original gathering in Colorado was to plant the seeds of intention to acquire this land as a home base for the Rainbow Family Tribe. This dream did not come to fruition and the Rainbow Gathering evolved into an annual weeklong nomadic festival held in a different national forest every summer.

Rainbow Gatherings are free, intentional community camping festivals that embody an egalitarian society with strong emphasis placed on shared resources and responsibilites. At the gathering, all labor and supplies are donated by the event's participants. The non-commercial nature of this event is supposed to legally guarantee the right to congregate on public land. The "focalizers" (a Rainbow term for the volunteer organizers who provide focus) consciously choose not to sign permits as a matter of principle, to exercise the freedom of assembly promised in the Bill of Rights and the First Amendment of the U.S. Constitution.[18]

Every summer during the first week of July, the national Rainbow Gathering draws up to 25,000 people from all over the country. Smaller regional gatherings are also held throughout the year, attended by many individuals who have fully embraced the lifestyle of "following the rainbow trail." A large contingent of

---

18 *According to the First Amendment to the Constitution of the United States of America: "Congress shall make no law… abridging the freedom of speech, or of the press, or the right of the people peaceably to assemble, and to petition the government for a redress of grievances."*

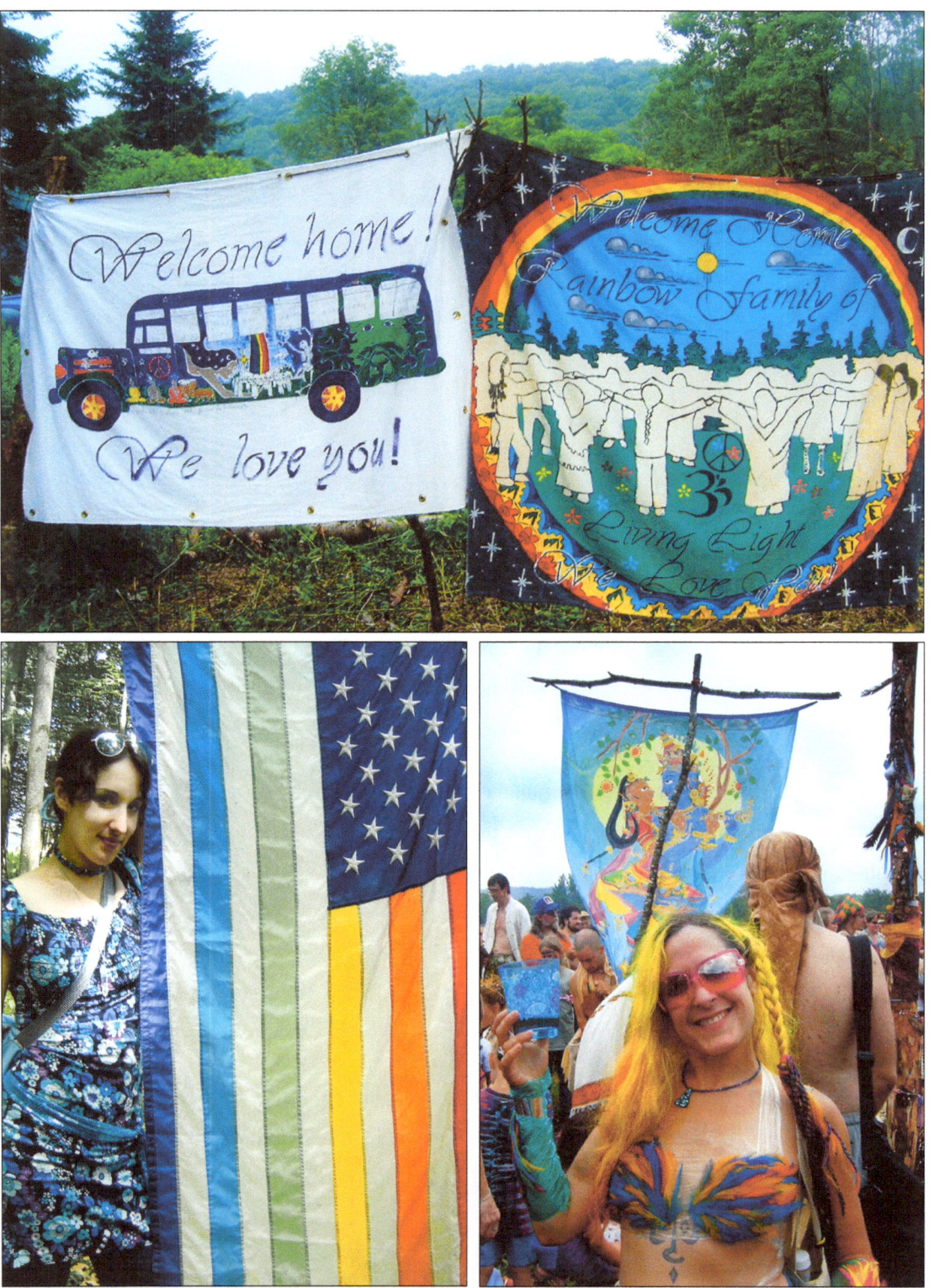

Let your freak flag fly! Rainbow Gathering, 2005

Rainbow Gathering attendees are deeply immersed in a nomadic culture, living out of ornately painted buses and vans, camping out in forests or on intentional community farms for much of the year. The Rainbow Gathering does not have ordained leaders, only self-appointed volunteers who take responsibility for the many tasks involved in setting up the infrastructure of a makeshift

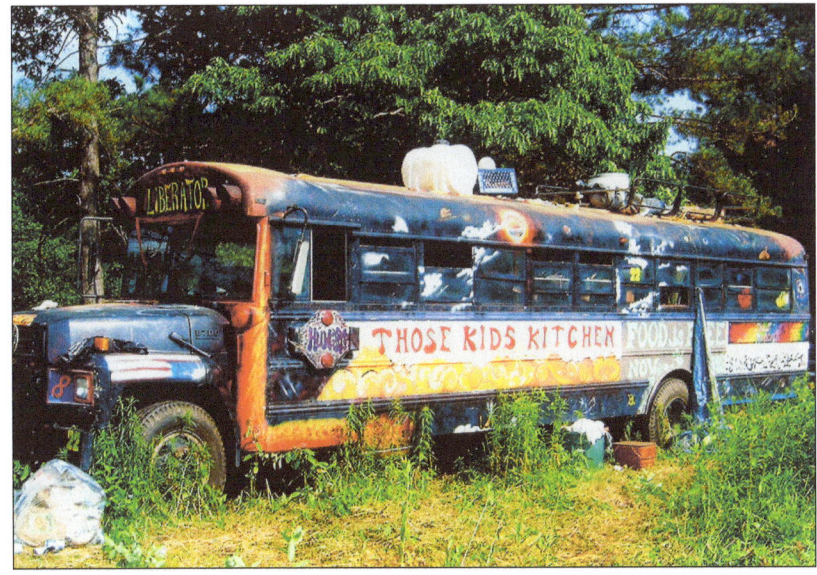

"Those Kids Kitchen" offered free meals throughout the week

city. This includes scouting and mapping the location, marking trails, building camp structures, installing water filtration systems, setting up free kitchens, dishwashing stations and eco-friendly bathrooms. The outstanding community effort involved in producing the annual gathering brings to life the old adage: many hands working together makes a tribe strong.

Cultivating a loving spiritual family is a central theme of the Rainbow Gathering. The gathering is a cross-generational affair that some attend with their entire clan, while others come to create an alternative family. Throughout the week, people greet each other in a familial fashion with: "welcome home" and refer to each other kindly as "brother" and "sister." While walking in the woods at a gathering, it is common to get stopped in a "hug zone" or stroll past a group of beautiful strangers that look at you and chant "Weeee Looovvvvve Youuuu!" (My posse of sarcastic New York City friends would jokingly respond back: "Weeee Tolerate Youuuuu!") The full name of the community that inhabits the gathering is: "Rainbow Family of Living Light." "Rainbow Family" indicates that all participants are kindred spirits from different walks of life, harboring an amalgamation of beliefs. Influences from Eastern mysticism, Christian theology, New Age and Native American mythology are all present at the gathering. "Living Light" refers to those who aim to be conscious channels for positive energy, while living a sustainable lifestyle in harmony with the natural world.

The Rainbow Family reveres the Earth as cherished Mother and sacred home. There is a mutual and complicit respect for the environment and an ingrained belief in the preservation of Earth's natural resources. In regards to trash, both the Rainbow Gathering and the Burning Man festival abide by the personal responsibility ethos of "you bring it in – you carry it out," and "leave no trace." There are no overflowing waste receptacles at either festival. Disposable products are highly discouraged. Garbage leaves the same way it comes in: in people's vehicles or on their backs. Most Rainbow Gatherings take place deep in the mountains and entail a laborious hike from the parking area to the campsite locations. These factors encourage people to travel light and live as organically as possible. The Rainbow Family is highly conscious about honoring fresh water as a valuable resource because it's an intrinsic element to survival that is not always easy to attain. Much of the water that sustains the gathering is retrieved from a sanctioned natural source. It is then brought back to camp and purified manually with a filter so it can be used for drinking, cooking, dish washing, and bathing.

Another core value that is shared by both the Burning Man festival and the Rainbow Gathering is the "no spectators" culture of radical self-expression. Effervescent creative culture thrives at the Rainbow Gathering with nightly performances, drum circles, costumed parardes, and workshops. The constraints of mainstream society are cast aside as people adorn themselves freely in neon-colored wigs, beaded jewelry, furry hats, face paint, sparkles, and mud. Some people take costuming a step further and transform themselves into sultry wood nymphs, flowered fairies, high priestesses, and shamanic hippie cowboys. For the duration of the festival, these mystical characters co-exist in whimsical encampments of handcrafted tree houses, psychedelic tapestries, brightly painted murals, dream catchers, altars, and shrines. Festivals that take place in remote natural locations lend themselves toward inspiring great ingenuity and resourcefulness. At the 2005 Rainbow Gathering, the New York City Purple Gang created a theater space from a tarp, a few logs, fabric, and tiki torches in order to host large communal meals and open mic cabaret nights. On

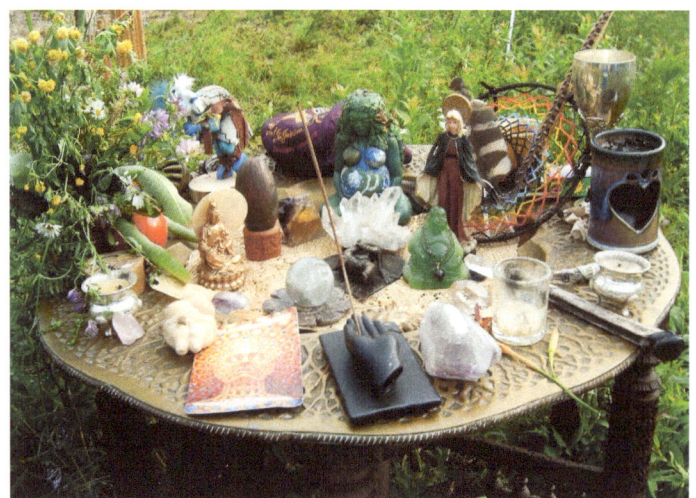

Rainbow Gathering altar, 2005

the final day of the gathering the Purple Gang extended their finest New York City hospitality and hosted the annual sushi and champagne brunch for over 450 people in their makeshift venue in the remote depths of the woods.

In July 2005, I embarked on a two-day road trip to the national Rainbow Gathering in West Virginia on the Bio Tour bus with DJ Arrow Chrome and crew. The Bio Tour traveled

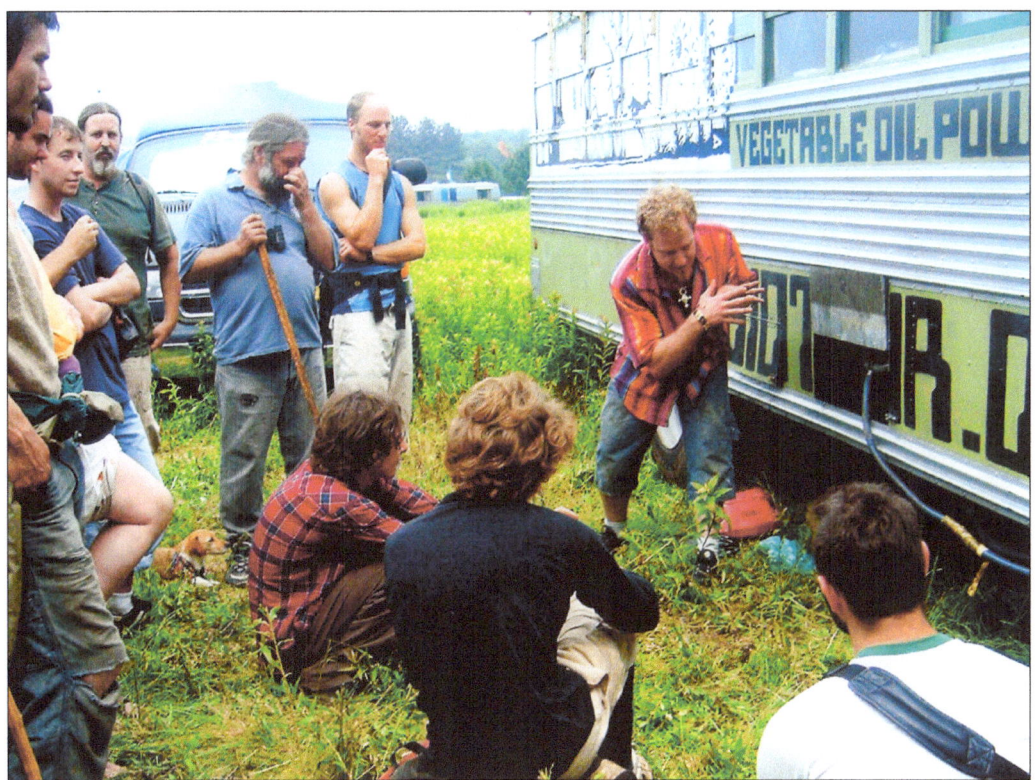

Arrow Chrome facilitates an alternative energy workshop at the Rainbow Gathering, West Virginia, 2005

to festivals all over the country to raise public awareness about global warming, alternative energy, and sustainable living. The centerpiece of the Bio Tour was a mural-covered bus that was fueled by solar panels, recycled vegetable oil, and biodiesel. On our journey to the gathering, the Bio Tour Rainbow crew stopped at local mom-and-pop restaurants to pick up used veggie oil to fuel the bus, pausing to answer curious bystanders' questions along the way. At the festival, Arrow Chrome taught workshops on how to convert diesel vehicles to run on veggie oil and highlighted the social and environmental benefits of finding viable alternatives to burning fossil fuels.

At the Rainbow Gathering, I was deeply moved by feelings of heightened intuitive awareness during my time immersed in the natural elements. While basking in the deep, quiet cloak of an endless canopy of trees, I realized how easy it is to lose sight of your own true nature and spiritual connection to others when habitually disconnected from the rhythms of the Earth. Modern society does not typically endorse communal living and as a by-product we become isolated by our own self-reliance. It was eye opening to witness how at the Rainbow Gathering communal activities and responsibilities took precedence over personal agendas, yet everyone's needs for food and shelter were met. Days revolved around preparing and

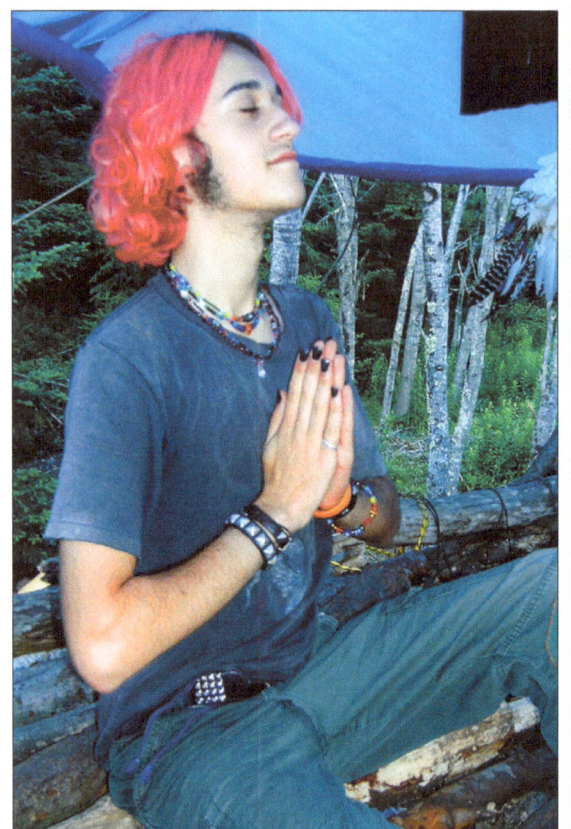

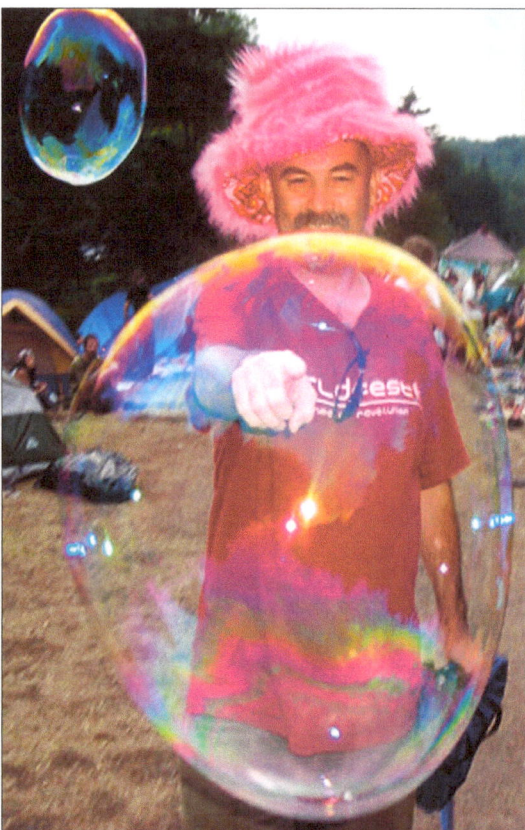

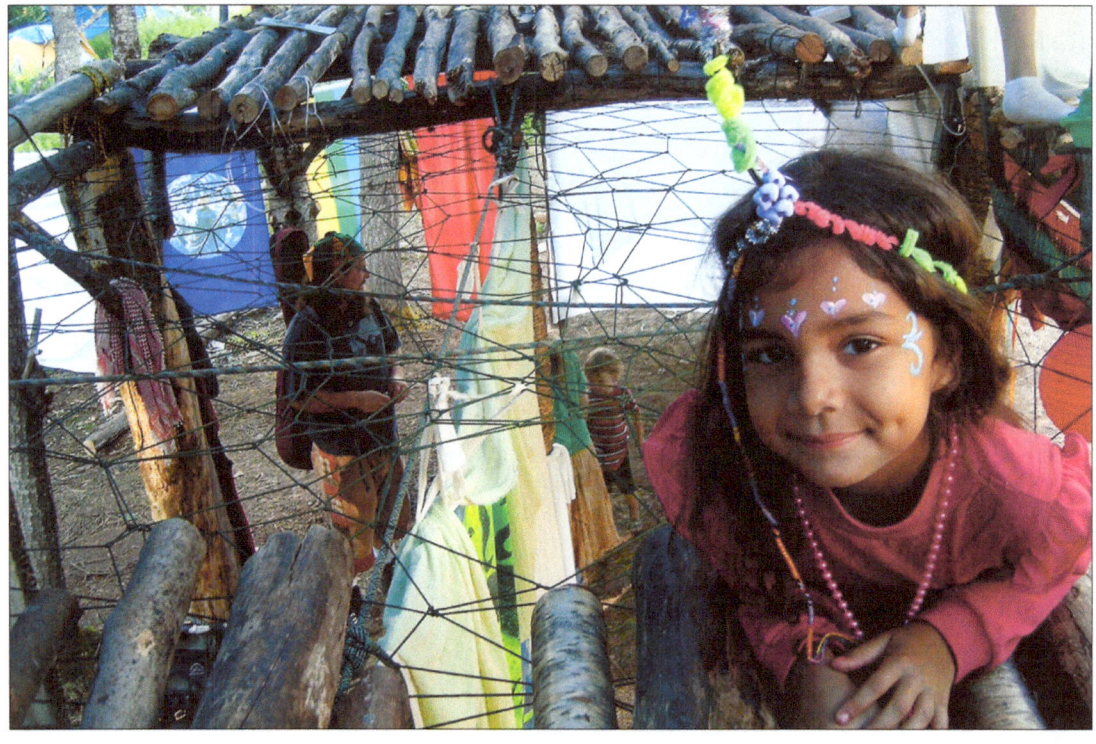

sharing meals, collectively maintaining the campsite, playing with children, telling stories, making music, exploring nature, and participating in holistic healing rituals.

Each year on the Fourth of July, The Rainbow Gathering culminates with the annual camp-wide ritual for world peace. On the morning of the fourth, silence reigns over the festival grounds as thousands of people engage in meditation and prayer for healing of all beings on planet Earth. At high noon the Rainbow Family congregates in the main meadow and forms a large circle, joining hands and hearts in silent communion. The ritual peaks as the silence is broken by the deep rumbling of thousands of people lifting their voices to the sky putting forth the universal chant "OMMMMMMM." A flock of children adorned with wreaths and flowers scamper out of the woods twirling colorful flags. They parade into the center of the circle, initiating the celebration that is to follow. The circle erupts as people run ecstatically into the center of the field toward a pole embellished with feathers, fabric, shells, and stones. For as far as the eye can see, revelers dance, drum, sing, and pray around the rainbow alter that serves as a beacon through which to channel world peace. Here, we learn that peace on Earth starts within ourselves. The love, light, and transformation experienced and shared at the Rainbow Gathering, belongs to each of us; we take it with us, and it grows.

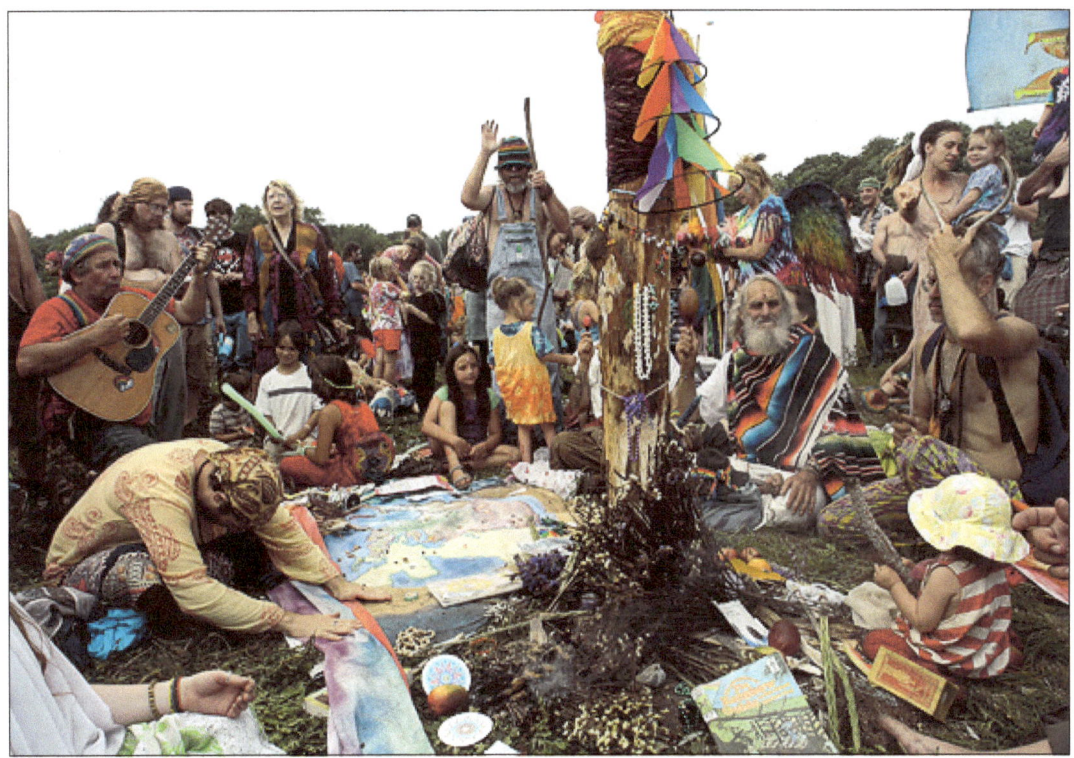

July 4th Ritual for World Peace, Rainbow Gathering, 2005

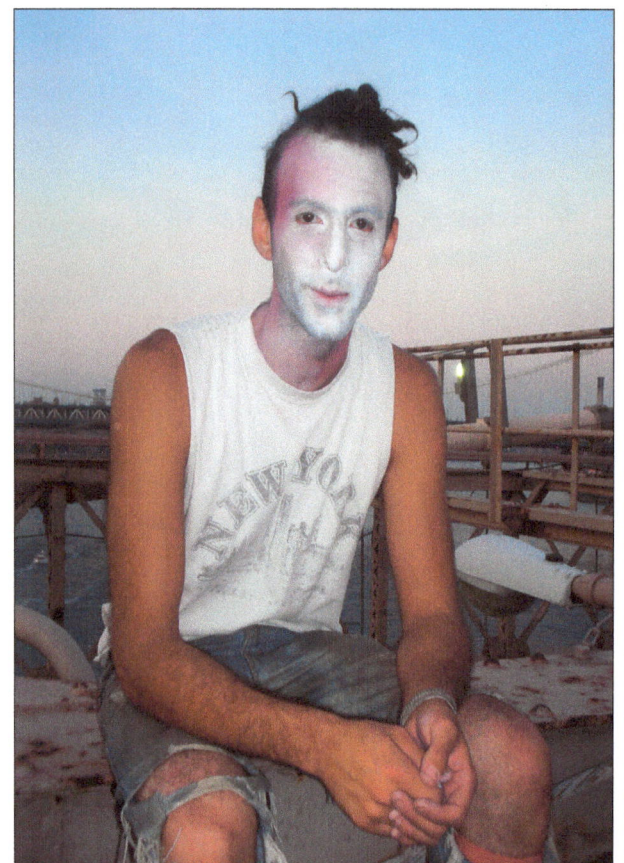
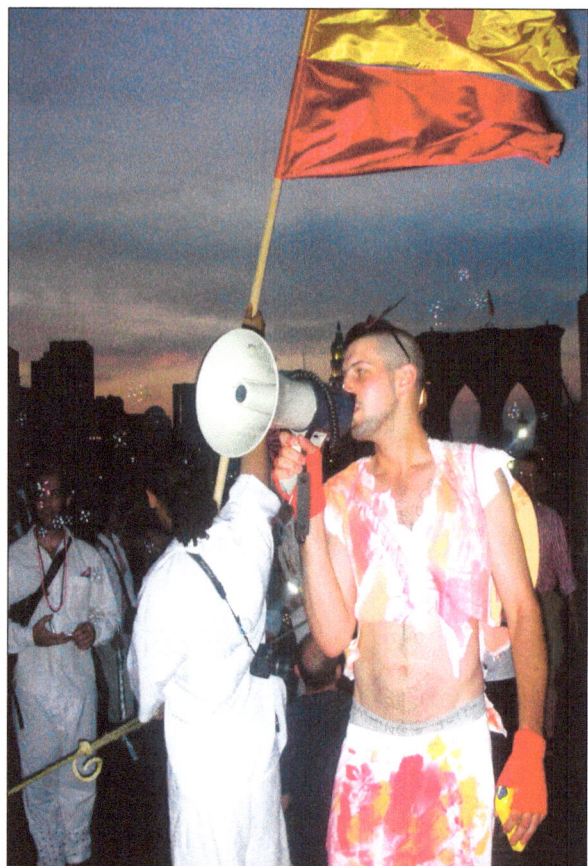
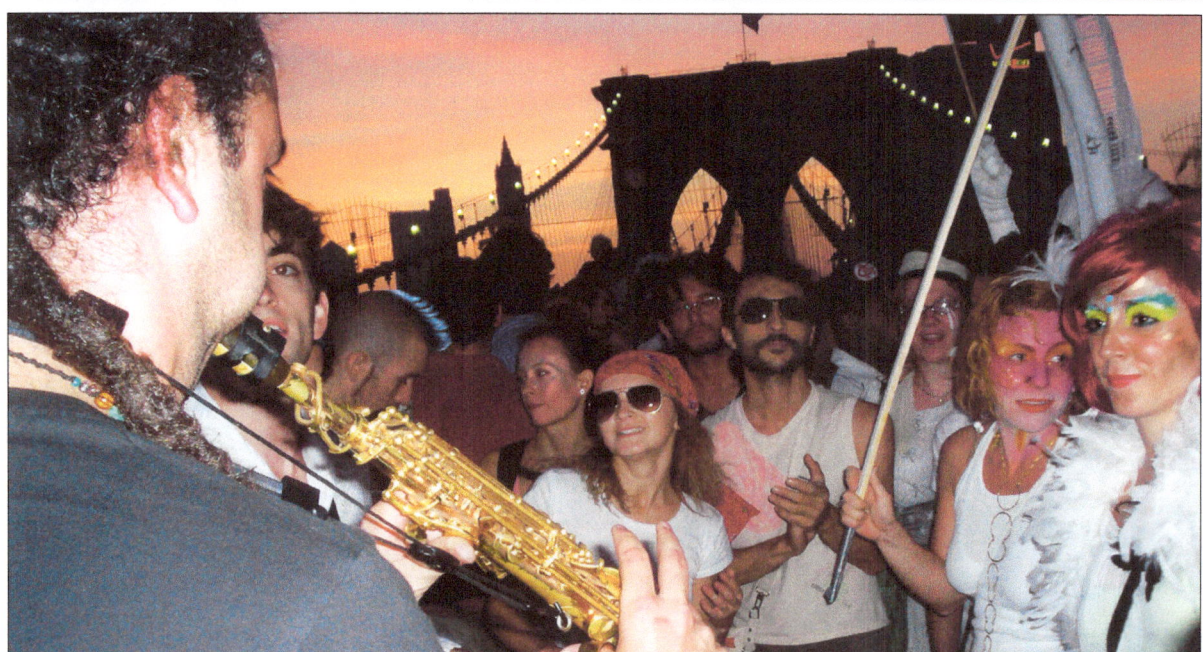

One Night of Fire parties on the Brooklyn Bridge, 2006-2007

ONE NIGHT OF FIRE

RENEGADE STREET PARTIES – 2005-2007

On a sultry summer night in New York City, three thousand festively-adorned revelers swarm the Brooklyn Bridge: Starlets, stilt walkers, angels, aerialists, and coaxers occupy the byways for as far as the eye can see. The melodic hum of bass drums echoes in the distance. The burgeoning crowd hovers on the bridge in eager anticipation. An unsuspecting bystander asks: "is today some sort of holiday?" A young woman holding a large red flag excitedly responds: "Today is Bastille Day!" As the sun sets over the city, a brass band begins to play. Horns, symbols and drums whip the crowd into an exuberant frenzy. A voice booms over a bullhorn into the crowd: "We are going to take Manhattan!" The flag-bearing coaxers swiftly guide the festooned flock off the Brooklyn Bridge and descend upon Manhattan to ignite One Night of Fire.

One Night of Fire was part of a trilogy of street parties celebrating liberation, creativity, and the unbridled soul of New York City. Renegade street parties are non-permitted, roving festivals: jubilant disruptions of mundane reality that employ unconventional uses of public space. The street (bridge, park, train, beach, or boardwalk) becomes the stage and dance floor, a liberated communal common ground in which free-flowing festivities take place. At first glance, renegade street parties may appear to be frivolous follies with flamboyant costumes and mad-hatter merriment, but their power lays in their active defiance against the established social order. It is an expression of freedom to openly play and create a shared cultural experience; live, immediate, and unfiltered. An intoxicating intimacy occurs when thousands of people participate in a joyous celebration, flowing in unison like blood in the veins of an enlivened city. Roving street parties are also a backlash against a shortage of large-scale venues available to alternative communities and are symbolic of an increasingly endangered culture that at times must defy all odds in order to congregate.

PARADES, PARTIES, AND PROTESTS

In the summer of 2004, the Republican National Convention invaded New York City in a further attempt to exploit 9/11 for political gain. Demonstrations were staged throughout the week of the convention to declare resistance to the Bush administration's corrupt military agenda. More than 1,500 activists were arrested for non-violent protest during the Republican National Convention (NYCLU, 2005). Democracy had failed (again). A deep-seated cultural malaise emerged in the aftermath of the RNC, swiftly followed by the nightmarish re-election of George W. Bush. Amidst the miasma, former Reclaim the Streets members William Etundi Jr. and Brad Will dreamed of ways to bring blood back to the streets of New York City, without the bloodshed. In the two years that followed, the renegade street parties First Warm Night and One Night of Fire were born.

First Warm Night and One Night of Fire were free public celebrations of uplifting, uninhibited arts culture at a time when New York City was increasingly overrun with regulations, gentrification, and surveillance. These mobile festivals were inspired by the Reclaim the Streets movement of the late 1990's, which had been responsible for numerous un-permitted carnival street parties held to protest corporate

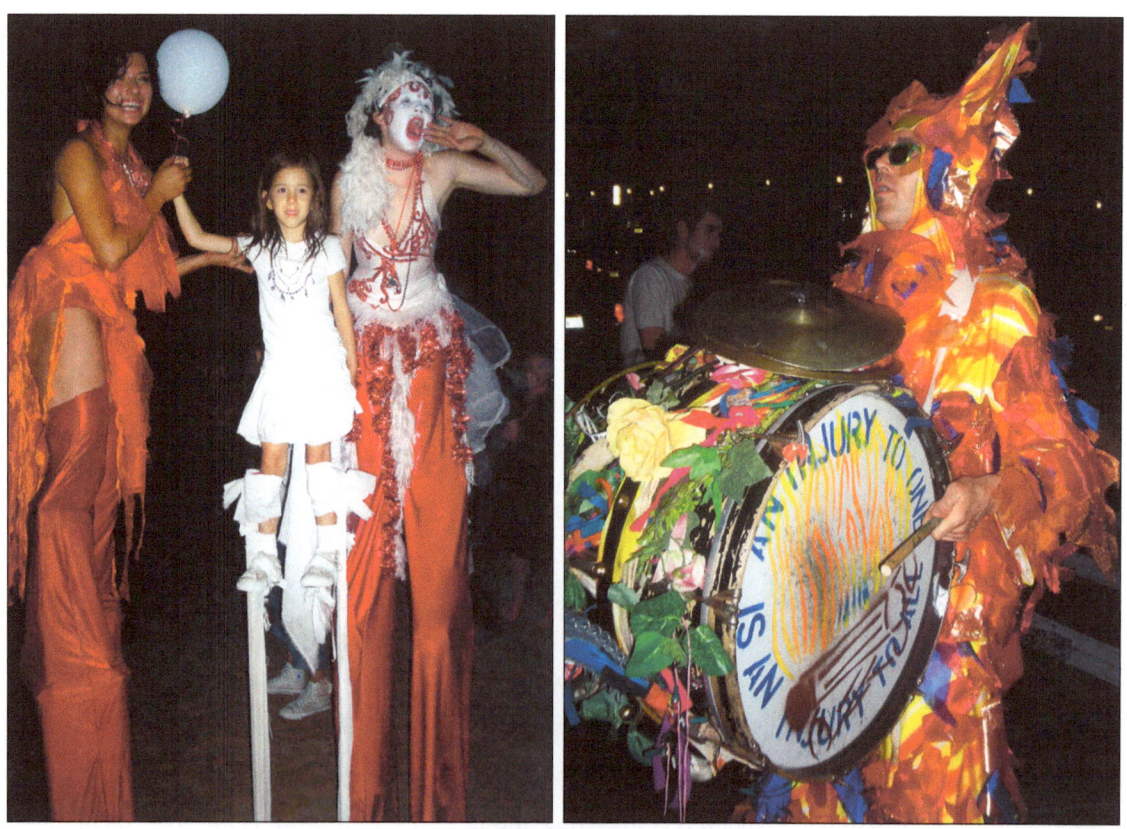

Coaxers and performers making public safety fun and fabulous, One Night of Fire, 2007

dominion and excessive privatization of the commons. At One Night of Fire, the emphasis on celebration and respect enabled the organizers to conduct positive interactions with the police and prevented the event from being immediately shut down. According to Will Etundi, founder of the Complacent Nation and the Danger collective: "We simply explained to the cops that we aren't anti-anything, we are pro-everything. We are artists celebrating the city we love, and they got it. At some points, it looked like the police were having as much fun as the rest of us."

In the winter of 2005, two-dozen organizers from an array of New York City art collectives joined forces to create First Warm Night, the first in a series of annual street parties. Their aim was to create an unpermitted, roving outdoor party on the first warm night of spring as a celebration of hope and renewal. At a time when cultural isolation prevailed, First Warm Night served as a catalyst for opening communication channels and strengthening ties amongst the grassroots artist community. In hindsight, many participants agreed that the highlight of the event was the weekly planning meetings attended by some of New York's finest renegade artist movers and

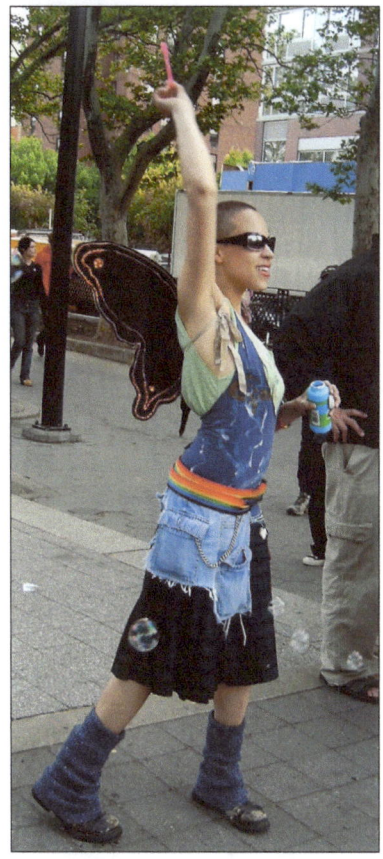

First Warm Night fairy coaxer at Chrystie Street Park, 2005

shakers. As First Warm Night drew closer, extended community meetings welcomed new participants and invited them to choose appropriate roles and share resources. When planning an event of this nature, organizers never know if the actual festivities will last for five hours or five minutes, but the most important outcome is that its inception brings people together.

In the months preceding First Warm Night, extensive collaboration was required to orchestrate the many facets of the roving festival, from the practical to the fantastical. This encompassed planning the party route, promoting the event, coordinating the visual art, performances and music for each location, and training the fairy coaxers. The First Warm Night coaxers were sparkly-winged volunteers who ushered the throngs of revelers through the streets of New York City to the various party destinations. Prior to the event, coaxers were trained to maintain public safety and interface with the police while guiding the massive crowds through the streets. To maintain the element of surprise and fend off being preemptively shut down, the party route and final destination remained a secret to the majority of

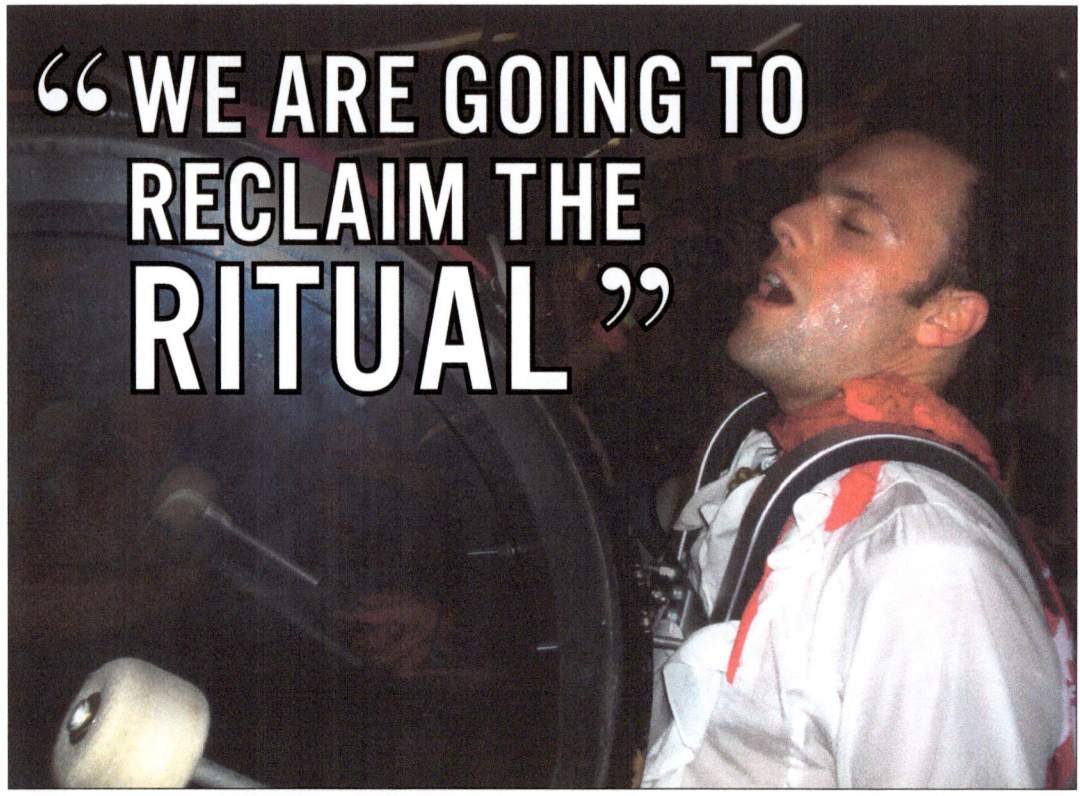

"WE ARE GOING TO RECLAIM THE RITUAL"

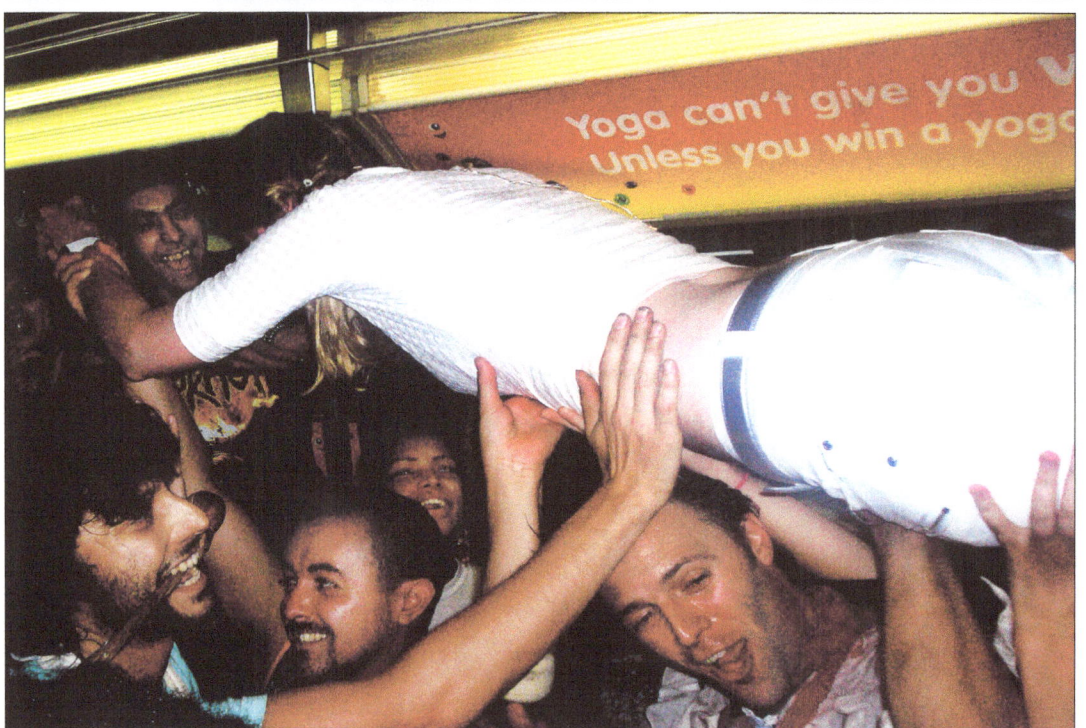

Ecstatic takeover of the New York City subway during One Night of Fire, 2007

the event's participants. First Warm Night revelers were required to be open to an unadulterated experience rich in surprise, spectacle, and spirit.

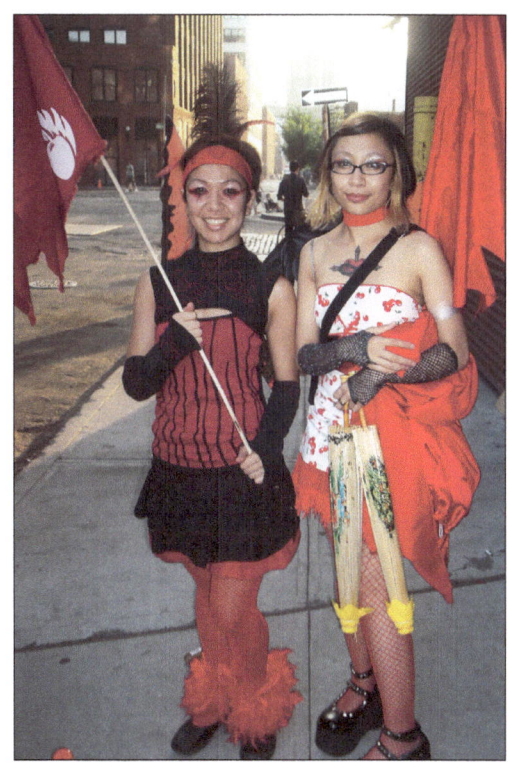

One Night of Fire, 2007

On a crisp spring afternoon in May 2005, hundreds of ebullient party people gathered in Chrystie Street Park in the Lower East Side in response to an alluring Internet message from Complacent.org: "Dozens of dedicated event makers have worked to lay the ground work. But this night is about you. Bring your performance, your music, your boom box and bass drums, bring your fire sticks, your stilts, public poetry and private passions, you are the performer and this is your stage. This is the night you dream of." After months of mystery surrounding the event, the night we had all been waiting for had finally arrived. As dusk fell, the crowd in the park grew denser and a heavy police presence appeared on the scene. Confusion permeated the air; no one knew what would happen next. Soon after, a bellowing voice rang out into the crowd: "To the F Train!" The fairy coaxers guided the massive crowd down into the Chrystie Street subway station where an exuberant train party ensued. As the train pulled into the station, the cars were immediately flooded with costumed revelers singing and dancing to music blaring from boom boxes, saxophones, cowbells, and drums. At the last stop, hundreds of colorful carousers spilled from the Smith and 9th Street train station and out onto the streets of Red Hook, Brooklyn.

The party procession paraded into a grassy park where it was greeted by an array of First Warm Night festivities: interactive games, balloons, ice cream, liquor, and an invigorating performance by the Hungry March Band. As the sun set, the marching band led the roaming party onto an industrial warehouse-lined backstreet adorned with colorful stenciled murals and performers dancing on elevated concrete platforms. A few blocks past the park, a flatbed truck toting a booming sound system joined the procession, heading up the massive flock of people dancing in the streets. At the height of the celebration, the NYPD attempted to halt the parade and shut the music down. Amidst the commotion, DJ Arrow Chrome got behind the decks, and started blasting the notorious Beastie Boys anthems "No Sleep 'Til Brooklyn" and "You Gotta Fight For Your Right To Party," sending the crowd into an ecstatic uproar.

PARADES, PARTIES, AND PROTESTS

Undeterred by the police, the party mass approached its final destination, a vacant waterfront pier overlooking the Statue of Liberty. Outside the entrance to the pier, a party bus with a Havok sound system blasted techno music while projecting psychedelic Feedbuck Galore video art onto an abandoned building. Throngs of revelers danced wildly in the streets while others casually cascaded onto the pier to take in the night's breathtaking view. Shortly after the crowd amassed, police helicopters began circling overhead and officers arrived on the scene to shut the party down. The bulk of the crowd dispersed and the remainder trickled into a nearby nightspot to celebrate the tail end of the First Warm Night.

"WE ARE ARTISTS CELEBRATING THE CITY WE LOVE"

In July 2006, the heat was turned up a notch in an effort to create a bigger and bolder renegade street party: "One Night of Fire." The element of fire was chosen to represent this event because it embodies passion, courage, creativity, and liberation. On a sweltering summer night at sunset, more than 2,000 people dressed in red converged on the Brooklyn Bridge. The premise: "The Battle for Brooklyn." As the enthusiastic crowd gathered, a circle of musicians drummed wildly as dynamic aerialist Akim Funk Buddah suspended himself from a rafter on the side of the bridge and proclaimed, "We are going to reclaim the ritual!" Akim's performance was followed by a tug-of-war competition between "Manhattan" and "Brooklyn" in order to decide what direction the roving party would take. Brooklyn kicked Manhattan's ass, and the festivities ensued. The flag-bearing coaxers directed the crowd off the bridge and into the streets of DUMBO Brooklyn. They entered a park where they were greeted by an enthusiastic "Stop Shopping" sermon from the Reverend Billy en route to the subway, followed by a boisterous train party out to Coney Island.

Upon arrival at Coney Island, thousands of glittering partygoers paraded in the streets, through the amusement park, and along the boardwalk as a cathartic ritual to uplift the spirits of this treasured, endangered landmark. The One Night of Fire procession culminated at the far end of the boardwalk, where the Bio Tour bus had parked and unleashed a throbbing sound system pumping electronic drum and bass music. A circle formed around several fire performers: poi spinners, fire breathers, and flaming hula-hoopers rhythmically gyrating to the pulsing beats. Moments later, a 10 foot tall phoenix effigy was set ablaze on the beach to symbolize the metaphor of hope and renewal associated with the mythical bird

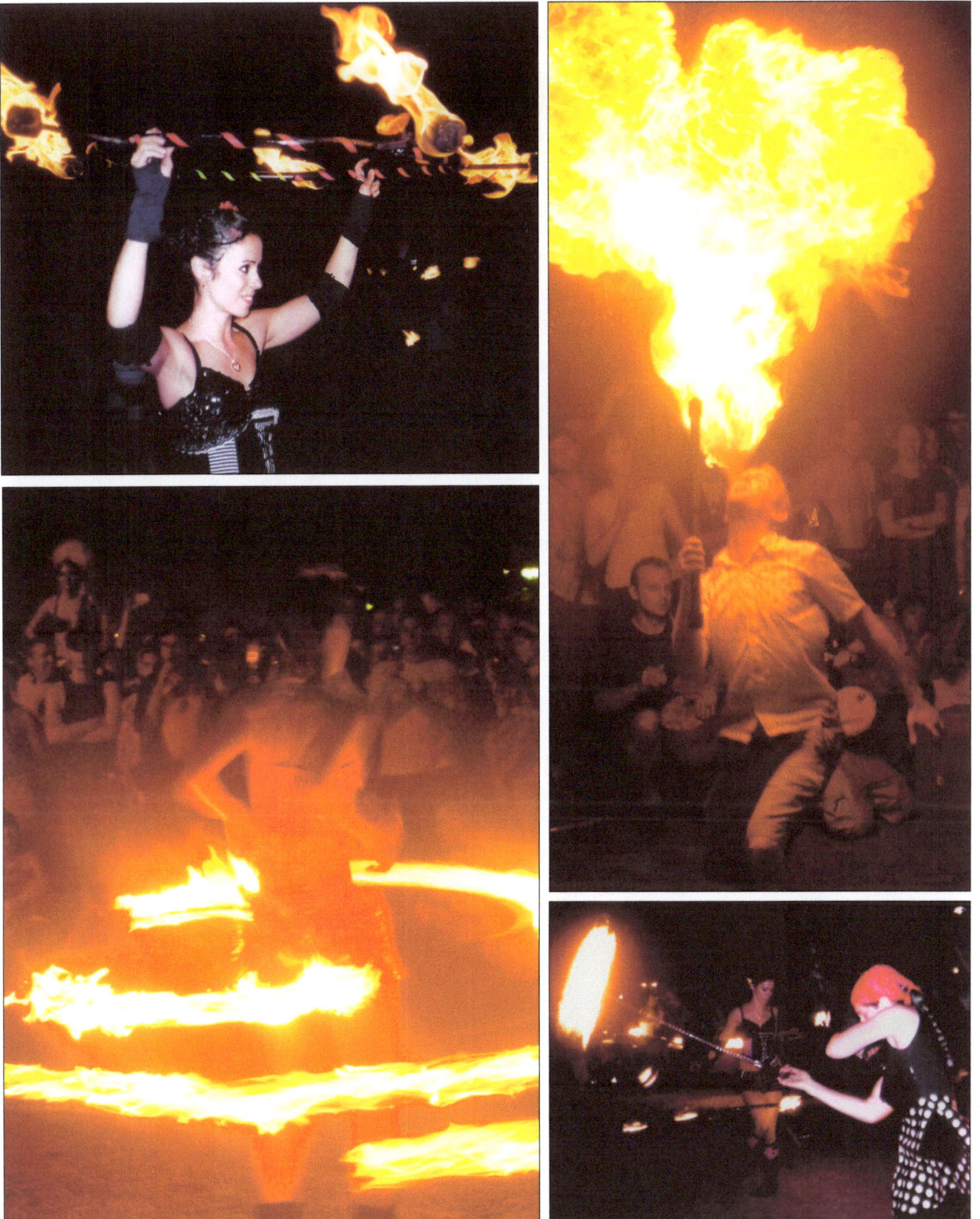

One Night of Fire performances at Coney Island, 2006 and 2007

rising from the ashes. This brazen ritual caught the attention of the police and they swarmed in to put a halt to the celebration. As the crowd began to disperse, dozens of party people piled into the Bio Tour Bus for a Johnny Cash sing-a-long and a ride back to DUMBO for the after party, blazing on through the sunrise.

The following year, in an emotional pre-event speech, organizer Will Etundi Jr. dedicated One Night of Fire 2007 to his fallen comrade, journalist Brad Will who was shot and killed in October 2006 while filming a teacher's strike in Oaxaca, Mexico. One Night of Fire 2007 was the city's most ambitious renegade street party to date, staged as a celebration of the spirit of New York City. In the days preceding the event, participants received messages via email or text with instructions: "Wear white, the more costumed the better. You are the angels that keep this city alive and untamed."

On July 14th 2007, more than 3,000 decked out party people gathered on the Brooklyn Bridge, paraded into City Hall Park, danced and drank in the fountains, witnessed a stunning stilting spectacle, and enacted a circus-style takeover of the New York City subway. The jubilant flock overwhelmed the NYPD with giddiness; enough that they opened the emergency exits and everyone got a free subway ride complete with marching bands, blaring boom boxes, alcohol-soaked cherries, train car body surfing, and sweaty new friends. Four full trains later, the mass arrived at the beloved, decrepit, historic home-to-the-freaks: Coney Island. On the Coney Island beach, the crowd celebrated with flames, drums, sparklers, skinny-dipping, and a mobile "clothes check" to boot. It was a party on the boardwalk, a party on the Wonder Wheel, a party on the side streets with local teenage contortionist break-dancers turning it out. An exquisite melding of the culture of Coney fused with the roving renegade street party. A beautiful night imprinted on my I-heart-New York 4-Ever. It is nights like these that keep my spirit alive. Thank you to everyone who is brave enough to step outside the box and create the world we dream to live in. You are my heroes.

CONCLUSION

The right to engage in non-violent civil disobedience as a means to impart social justice is one of the primary ideologies upon which American democracy was founded. Despite a rich tradition of resistance and dissent in the U.S., activists often encounter harsh opposition from the entrenched powers-that-be and face an escalating risk of becoming victims of police brutality. Corporate-driven policies deepen inequalities and distance the government from the will of the people they are supposed to represent. Worse still, an alienated political class that is afraid of its own citizens often resorts to the increased use of a militarized police force to crush non-violent protests. Meanwhile the mass media frequently under-represents significant political demonstrations and commonly portrays activists as hysterical nuisances, failing to convey their bravery and positive contributions that benefit society as a whole. Many facets of culture as we know it would be subject to far greater inequality if citizens had not exercised the right to protest.

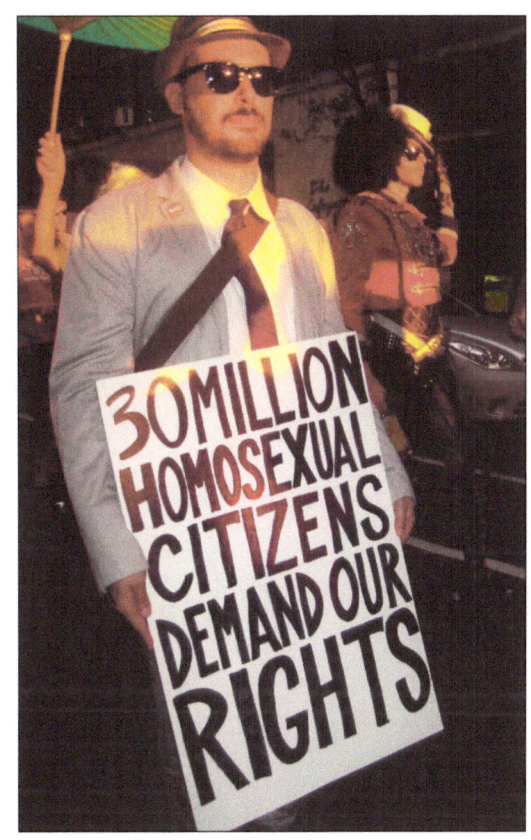

Drag March, New York City, 2008

Throughout U.S. history, activists have worked diligently to make the founding promises of American democracy a reality; from the birth of the Declaration of Independence, to the recent mobilizations against unbridled corporate greed and war, to the abolition of slavery, the fight for racial equality, women's rights, worker's rights, gay rights, immigrant rights, and for the sake of cultivating a working democracy – these movements continue to evolve today. A successful democracy requires active participation. It is our right and responsibility to educate ourselves on current events, to vote, and to petition our representatives when

99

faced with injustice. According to the late Senator Robert Byrd, "There is a power which can serve as a check against abuses of power by a government… that is the power of the informed citizen – one who has read enough, who understands enough, who has developed a base of knowledge against which to judge truth from falsehood … an informed citizenry has to participate, ask questions, and demand answers and accountability to make a country like ours work" (Lampord, 2004:5).

While it is important to develop dialogue with our political representatives, there will be times when leaders have agendas that do not serve the interests of their constituents. When our government and other long-standing institutions fail us, we must be empowered to roll up our sleeves and do the relief work ourselves. We are on a tectonic fault line in human existence. Things are changing faster then ever before. Planet Earth is reeling from a destructive phase of industrial plundering that has depleted vast natural resources and poisoned its inhabitants. While we ignore our interconnected relationship to the Earth, our society has become plagued by cancer and mental illness. We can no longer afford to sit back passively and wait for the government to fix all of the looming problems. All of us need to step up and participate in cultivating a sustainable and uplifting paradigm shift. We are inventing the future.

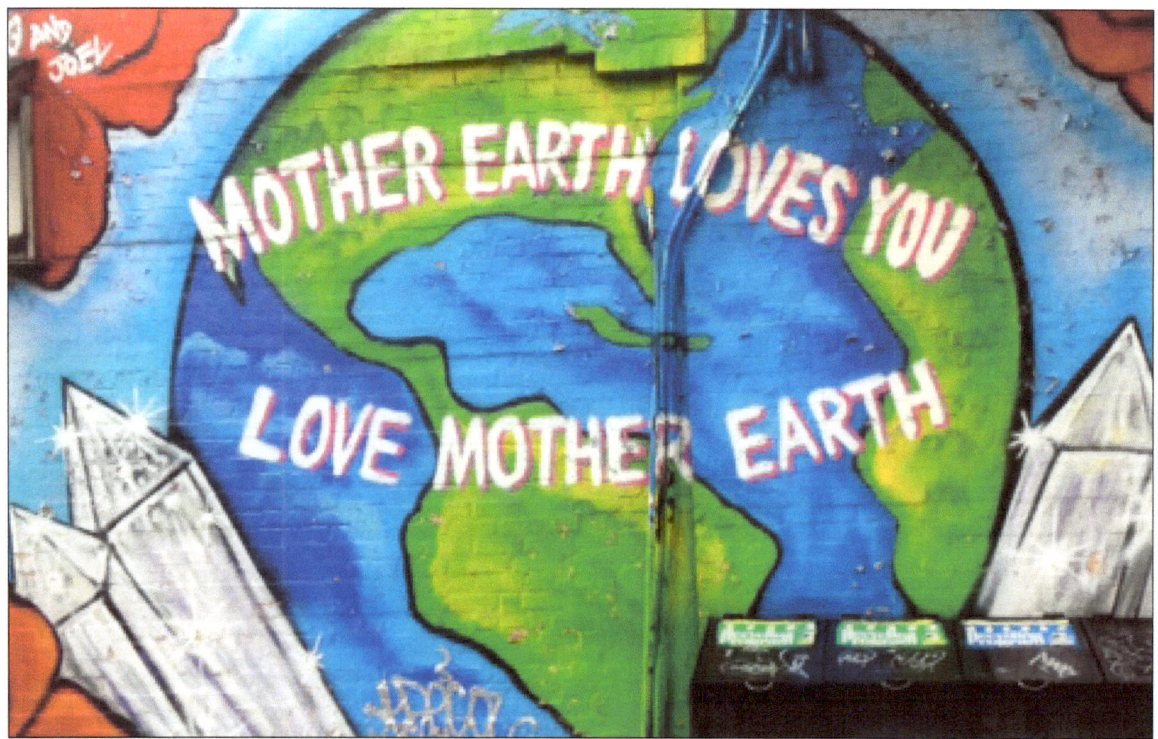

East Village street art, New York City, 2012

Parades, Parties, and Protests aims to combat the apathy and disillusionment of our times by exposing critical social and political issues from the perspective of diverse creative dissent movements. I hope this book will inspire its readers to be agents of uplifting transformation in society and in their personal lives. Being an effective ambassador of change is not just about signing petitions and parading in the streets. In its most potent form, activism is integrated into the lifestyle choices we make on a daily basis. There are many positive steps we can take toward catalyzing a paradigm shift, starting with reclaiming our mental space and turning off the television: by reducing consumption and increasing recycling, by minimizing the use of disposable plastic bottles and shopping bags; by using public transportation, bikes, and carpooling to reduce dependency on fossil fuels; by growing our own food and avoiding GMOs; by supporting artists and independent businesses; by having informed conversations and cultivating households, businesses and relationships that uphold environmental sustainability, compassion, and respect for all.

I extend my utmost gratitude to the activists throughout history that fought for the liberties we have today, and to the brave souls that continually strive to preserve those liberties and push society to evolve further. There is power in numbers! Support movements that are aligned with your core beliefs. Live with integrity and do what you love as much as possible. Use your dollar as your vote. Megacorporations will lose their tyrannical stranglehold if we refuse to consume their products. We can take conscious steps to reclaim the sovereignty we deserve and strengthen our communities by investing in what we believe in, sharing resources, and launching entrepreneurial endeavors that embody the ethos of a more humane and just world. Standing up for what you believe and living by example are the primary ways of generating positive change. In the words of the late Mahatma Gandhi, "You must be the change you wish to see in the world." The choice is ours. Peace.

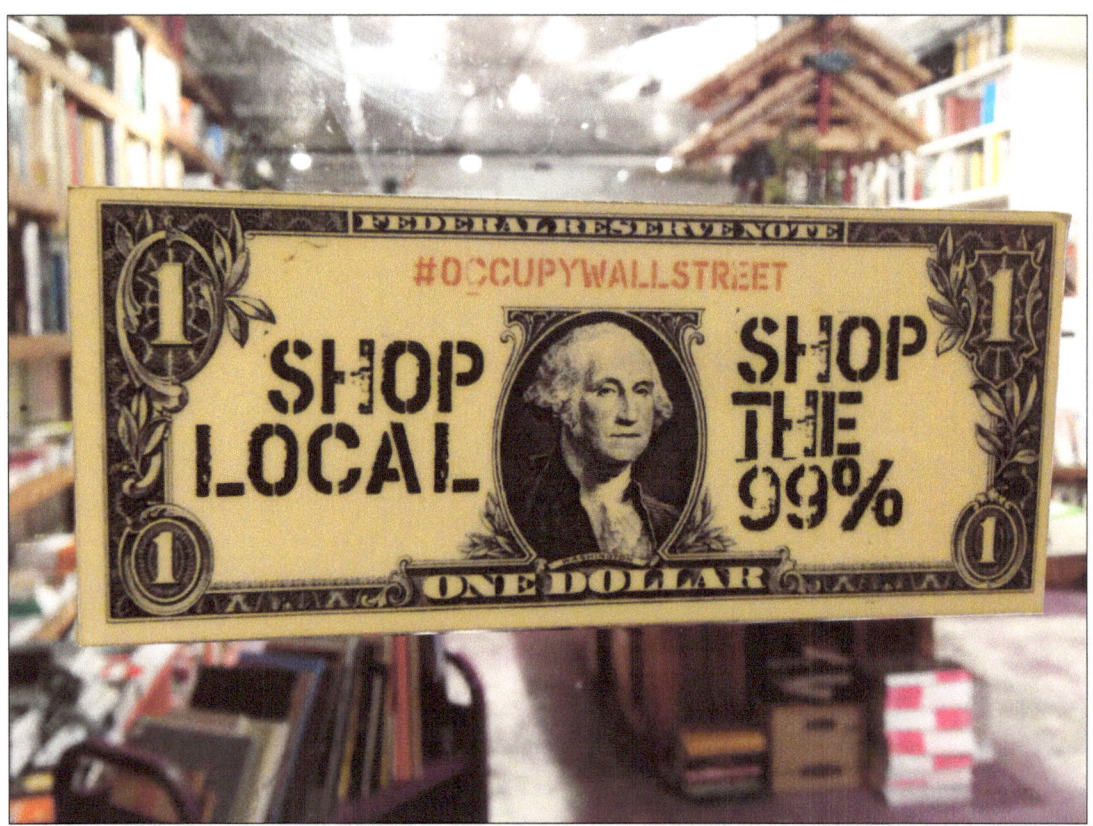

"Shop local" Brooklyn, New York, 2013

AUTHOR'S NOTE

The first decade of the 21st century was like a tidal wave, leaving in its wake a ravaged social landscape wrought by turmoil. As the state of global affairs grew more daunting, I needed to create a testimonial baring witness to the devastation and glorious moments of rebirth that occurred during this turbulent time. My original intention for producing *Parades, Parties, and Protests* was to make a tool for mobilization against the Bush administration and the Iraq war, and to aid the corresponding culture of resistance in making its mark on history. This record-breaking protest movement had gone largely unnoticed by many due to the mass media's glaring lack of coverage. I was intensely driven by the desire to create a platform for broadcasting the dissenting voices being overtly ignored by the mass media and the government. When referring to the Iraq war in hindsight, many politicians now fumble and say: "We didn't know, we were misled." They should have listened to their constituents. When future generations look back in dismay and ask why Americans didn't try to stop the Iraq war, this book is a testament to the fact that millions of people stood up and said "NO!"

9/11 served as the catalyst for the Bush administration's invasion of Iraq, an atrocity that resulted in hundreds of thousands of violent deaths and trillions of dollars in U.S. national debt. As the insidious neo-con think tank Project For the New American Century had plotted in the previous decade, the U.S. government siphoned off the majority of the country's resources for invasive surveillance and war in the name of "national security." The U.S. government made great efforts to silence opposition to its militaristic agenda. The mass media was complicit in facilitating this agenda by disseminating biased information that came out of the White House, despite the fact that President Bush and his policies were among the most unpopular in U.S. history. Simultaneously, the Iraq war mobilized millions of people around the globe to participate in the largest peace movement in modern history. The fact that these efforts could not prevent the war reflects the failure of American democracy and the entrenched power of U.S. militarism.

In post-9/11 America, the on-going erosion of civil liberties has become the major plight of the new millennium. The rights of freedom of speech, privacy peaceful assembly, freedom of the press and due process are increasingly under fire. Public spaces are drastically reduced in an effort to maximize profits and exercise social control. When in public, we are subject to a barrage of restrictive regulations and are under surveillance at all times. We are constantly encouraged to be fearful and to consume. Opportunities for creating culture outside the realm of commerce are increasingly diminished, as the majority of sanctioned socializing is relegated to venues designed to generate corporate profits. However, a positive shift is underway. The past few years has seen a huge upsurge in self-publishing, blogging, alternative news reporting and independent fundraising for the arts. Now, protest images reach millions of people around the globe when they are broadcast through social media and online news sources. After decades of being shut out of mass media, people are finding innovative ways to participate in the dissemination of opinions and information – an integral component in cultivating a working democracy.

At the close of 2008, the U.S. experienced a major financial crisis, with a fall out so far-reaching that the world plummeted into a global recession. People were forced to lower their standards of living out of sheer necessity. However, some facets of the recession were a blessing in disguise. Reversing the course of rampant consumerism is essential for life on Earth to survive. Hyper-industrial capitalism has generated a gaping hole in the ozone layer, climate change, the depletion of non-renewable natural resources, raging cancer epidemics, and irreversible species extinction. Our government and business leaders make decisions as if they have another planet to go live on when they are done plundering this one. Strict regulations must be enforced that mandate corporations to drastically reduce industrial pollution, and local municipalities to implement high functioning waste reduction and recycling programs. In turn, the U.S. government must divert resources away from war and other destructive endeavors and redirect tax dollars toward building a sustainable green infrastructure. Now is the time to cultivate stewardship of the planet and to restore balance in the natural world. Our quality of life and the wellbeing of future generations depends on the course of action we take now.

A large portion of *Parades, Parties, and Protests* is an intimate exploration of New York City, the cultural epicenter of the 9/11 aftermath. My pride as a fourth-generation New Yorker inspires me to tell lesser-known stories of the city I love that occurred during a time of massive change and upheaval. Bearing witness and sharing this story helps to prevent a significant moment in history from fading into obscurity. In New York City, the recent past often becomes a distant memory because the city is a transient international hub brimming with intense sensory overload and sprawling gentrification. Rich cultural history is paved over by rampant commercialism, with treasured landmarks sold off to the highest bidder. In February 2009,

THE RICH REALLY ARE GETTING RICHER ... "BETWEEN 1979 AND 2007, THE TOP ONE PERCENT OF AMERICANS HAVE SEEN INCOMES GROW BY AN AVERAGE OF 275 PERCENT"

— CONGRESSIONAL BUDGET OFFICE

billionaire Mayor Michael Bloomberg hosted a luncheon for wealthy developers at the Grand Hyatt hotel to discuss the future of New York City. A group of informed citizens infiltrated this exclusive meeting and staged a boisterous protest to express their indignation with being excluded from a major decision making process regarding their communities. One protester, Ms. Imasuen shouted: "We don't have a voice, we're not at the table and we demand to be at the table. We demand that the mayor gives us a meeting, not for corporate America to decide the fate of all New Yorkers" (Santos, 2009).

In a bold attempt to buck the entrenched power of corporate dominion, the Occupy Wall street movement was born on September 17, 2011 in the heart of New York City. A call to action published in Adbusters magazine prompted close to a thousand people to set up camp at Zuccotti Park in Manhattan's financial district. They pitched tents and joined forces to protest multinational corporations degrading influence over the democratic process, and to demand the prosecution of the bankers responsible for the devastating 2008 economic collapse. "Banks got bailed out – We got sold out!" was a popular chant at Occupy demonstrations that expressed deep outrage over the multi-billion dollar bailouts given to corporations responsible for the meltdown. These institutions in turn gave millions of dollars in bonuses to wealthy executives, while many Americans were faced with foreclosure, record-high unemployment and exponentially increasing costs of living. Inspired by popular uprisings in Tunisia and Egypt's Tahrir Square, the Occupy movement was a sweeping public outcry against insidious corporate greed, burgeoning income inequality, and white-collar crime. A cornerstone slogan of the Occupy movement is: "We are the 99 percent," which refers to the uneven distribution of the wealth between the majority of the population versus the wealthiest one percent – the obscenely rich elite minority who write the exploitative rules and profit from an unjust global economy.[19]

---

19 *A new report from the Congressional Budget Office (CBO) appears to have confirmed that the rich really are getting richer. Between 1979 and 2007, the top 1% of Americans with the highest incomes have seen their incomes grow by an average of 275%, according to the study (CBO, 2011).*

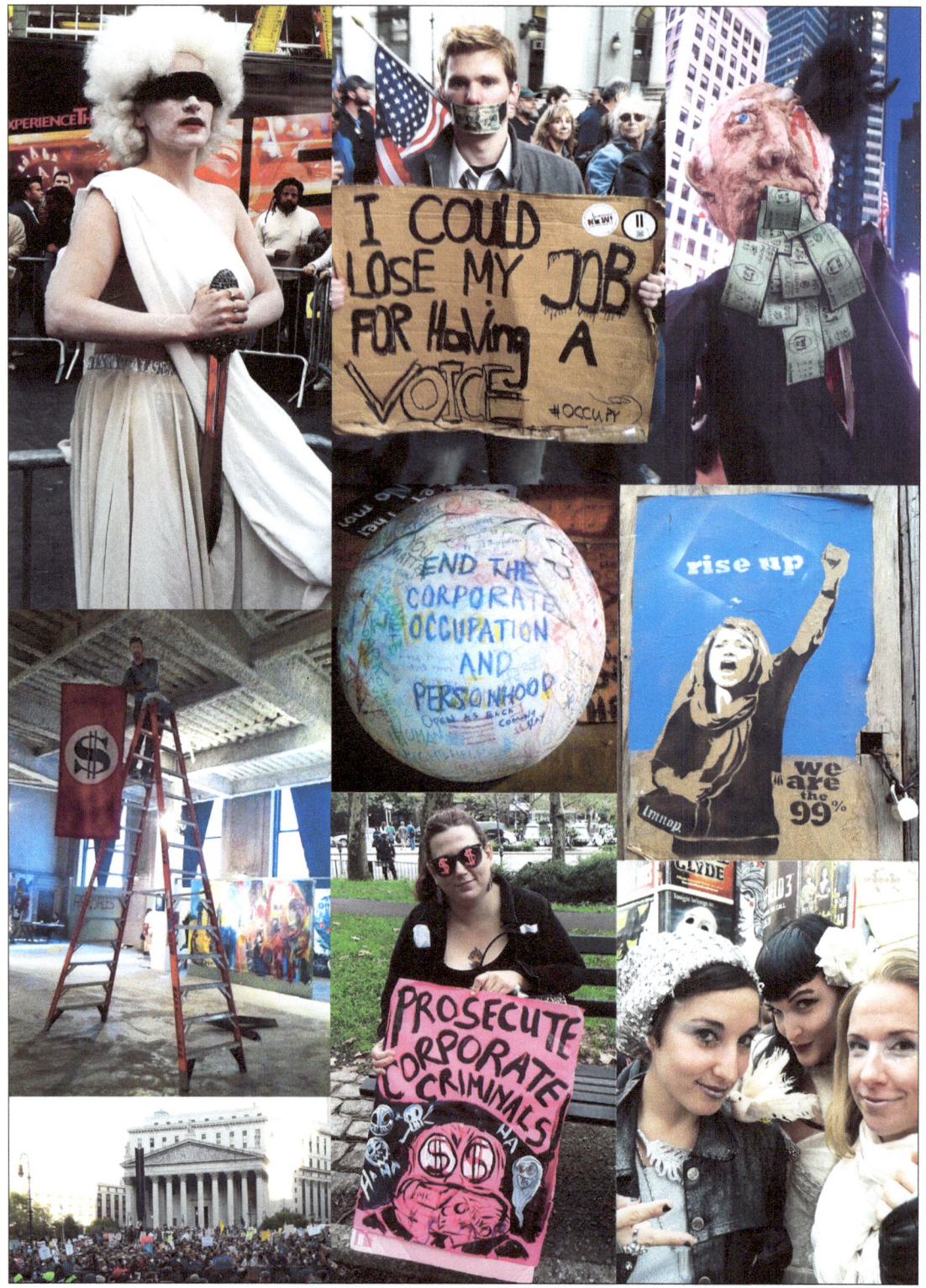

Occupy Wall Street protests, New York City, 2011

For two solid months, thousands of activists participated in a peaceful occupation of Zuccotti Park, with many camping out for weeks in the highly-publicized tent city. The park was renamed "Liberty Square" by the occupiers and was temporarily transformed into a small village with a kitchen, a library, and a media center where the Occupy press team ran websites, live video streams, and updates on social networks through which they documented and promoted the ongoing protests. As the Occupy movement gained greater visibility, protests spread like wildfire all over the city. There were daily marches in the financial district, public assemblies in Liberty Square, Union Square, and Washington Square Park, art exhibitions in numerous locations, and large demonstrations at City Hall and in Times Square. On October 1st, 2011 more than 700 people were arrested during a march across the Brooklyn Bridge. Armed with communication technology, protesters documented the mass arrests on the ramp below while shouting at the police officers: "The whole world is watching!" And it was. The Occupy protests in New York City inspired a global movement that spread to over 100 cities in the United States and actions in over 1,500 cities around the world (OWS, 2011).

In November 2011, Occupy encampments around the nation were confronted with violent evictions. In New York City Mayor Bloomberg authorized "his army" – the NYPD – to use military force to remove non-violent protesters from Zuccotti Park (Walker, 2011). Shortly after midnight on November 15th, police in riot gear stormed the park and destroyed activists' possessions, inflicted serious physical injuries, and arrested more than 200 people. Freedom of the press was suspended as police denied credentialed members of the media access to the vicinity, and many were forcefully prevented from documenting the eviction. While the raid was underway, the Occupy Wall Street Media Team issued an official response: "You can't evict an idea whose time has come" (OWS, 2011). At the close of 2011 – a year marked by civil unrest and social upheaval – Time magazine declared "The Protester" person of the year in honor of the millions of people around the world (in Egypt, Spain, Greece, London, New York, Oakland, Los Angeles, and beyond) who took to the streets to protest corrupt governments and financial institutions. The citizens of the world are waking up. This is just the beginning.

Parades, Parties, and Protests highlights beauty amidst dark times, delving into creative forms of protest that embody the power of art and community to heal, transform, and propel society into the future. Over the past decade, I have found joy and liberation in urban gardens, gritty warehouse parties, roving street festivals, and national gatherings in remote deserts and forests. During an era marked by corruption and strife, these were the cherished moments that made life worth living, and ultimately give me hope for better times to come.

Sarah Sparkles

BIBLIOGRAPHY

Adorno, Theodor, and Max Horkheimer. The Dialectic of Enlightenment. New York: Continuum, 1995. Chapter: The Culture Industry: Enlightenment as Mass Deception.

Al Jazeera, "Iraq and US Sign Forces Agreement." Retrieved November 21, 2008. http://www.aljazeera.com.

Al Jazeera, "Inside Story America: Which Stories Did the Media Ignore This Year?" Retrieved January 5, 2013. http://www.aljazeera.com.

"Basic Documents Pertaining to Human Rights in the Inter-American System." American Convention on Human Rights, O.A.S. Treaty Series. Series no. 36 (1992): p. 17.

Baum, Dan. New York Times, "Nation Builders for Hire." Last modified June 22, 2003. Retrieved May 20, 2012. http://www.nytimes.com.

BBC News, "Iraq war illegal, says Annan." Last modified September 16, 2004. Retrieved May 5, 2005. http://news.bbc.co.uk.

Bell, John. "Louder Than Traffic." Radical Street Performances. Edited by Jan Cohen-Cruz. London and New York: Routledge, 1998. p. 271-280.

Berger, John. The Successes and Failures of Picasso. New York: Pantheon Books, 1965. p. 164-165.

Burning Man, "What is Burning Man? Timeline." Retrieved July 14, 2008. http://www.burningman.com.

Cohen-Cruz, Jan. Radical Street Performances. London and New York: Routledge, 1998. p. 65.

Congressional Budget Office, "Trends in the Distribution of Household Income Between 1979 and 2007." Last modified October 25, 2011. Retrieved May 1, 2012. http://cbo.gov.

Doig, Will. Metro Weekly, "Squeeze Play: RAVE Act Slips through Senate in Amber Alert Bill, Heads to White House." Last modified April 17. 2003. Retrieved May 5, 2004. http://www.metroweekly.com.

Donnelly, Thomas. The Project for the New American Century, "Rebuilding America's Defenses." Retrieved December 9, 2004. http://newamericancentury.org.

Durham, Meenakashi, and Douglas Kellner. Media and Cultural Studies. Malden, MA: Blackwell Publishing, 2001.

Rep. Emanuel (IL), Rep. Gutierrez (IL), and Rep. DeGette (CO). Iraq Debate Transcript. Congressional Record H63. Retrieved March 16, 2007. http://www.truemajorityaction.org.

Federal Election Commission. "2000 Presidential General Election Results." Retrieved September 5, 2003. http://www.fec.gov.

Falk, Richard. Al Jazeera, "Kuala Lumpur tribunal: Bush and Blair guilty." Last modified November 28, 2011. Retrieved May 1, 2012.

Fisher, William. Inter Press Service, "U.S./Iraq: Report Finds 'Appalling Level of Fraud and Greed'." Last modified June 29. 2005. Retrieved August 31, 2005. http://ipsnews.net.

Golden, Daniel, James Bandler, and Marcus Walker. "Bin Laden Family Could Profit From a Jump In Defense Spending Due to Ties to U.S. Bank." The Wall Street Journal, September 27, 2001.

Herbert, Bob. New York Times, "Ultimate Insiders." Last modified April 14, 2003. Retrieved June 11. 2004. http://www.nytimes.com.

Iraq Body Count, "Documented civilian deaths from violence." Retrieved January 5, 2012. http://www.iraqbodycount.org.

Kuhner, Jeffrey T. The Washington Times. "Obama's Power Grab Executive Order Expands Presidential Perogative." Last modified March 22, 2012. Retrieved April 15, 2012. http://www.washingtontimes.com.

Labaton, Stephen. New York Times. "Deregulating the Media: The Overview; Regulators Ease Rules Governing Media Ownership. Last modified June 3, 2003. Retrieved January 8, 2004. http://www.nytimes.com.

Lampord, Nicole and James Mann. Peace Signs: The Anti War Movement Illustrated. New York: Edition, 2004. p. 5.

Lasn, Kalle. Culture Jam. New York: Quill Harper Collins, 1999. p 25-26 67-68, 186-187.

Madsen, Wayne. In These Times. "Questionable Ties: Tracking bin Laden's money flow leads back to Midland, Texas." Retrieved June 4, 2003. http://www.inthesetimes.com.

Marx, Karl, and Friedriech Engels. "The Ruling Class and the Ruling Ideas." Media and Cultural Studies. Edited by Meenakashi Durham and Douglas Kellner. Malden, MA: Blackwell Publishing, 2001. p. 39-42.

McCarthy, Timothy and John McMillian. The Radical Reader. New York: New Press, 2003. p. 351.

Mikalbrown, Kerstin. "Saving Esperanza Garden: the struggle over community gardens in New York City." From ACT-UP to the WTO. Edited by Ben Shepard and Ronald Hayduk. London and New York: Verso, 2002. p. 229-233.

Miller, T. Christian. Blood Money: Wasted Billions, Lost Lives and Corporate Greed in Iraq. New York: Little, Brown and Company - Hachette Book Group, 2006.

MSNBC, "Most oppose more troops in Iraq." Last modified January 11, 2007. Retrieved March 16, 2007. http://www.msnbc.msn.com.

New York Civil Liberties Union, "Rights and Wrongs at the RNC: A Special Report about Police and Protest at the Republican National Convention." Retrieved July 18, 2006. http://www.nyclu.org.

Occupy Wall Street, "You Can't Evict an Idea Whose Time Has Come." Last modified November 15, 2011. Retrieved January 8, 2012. http://occupywallst.org.

Open Congress. "Congressional actions regarding President Bush's 2007 proposed troop "surge" in Iraq." Retrieved May 5, 2007. http://www.opencongress.org.

PBS, "Excerpts from 1992 Draft 'Defense Planning Guidance'." Retrieved June 5, 2004. http://www.pbs.org.

Purdum, Todd. New York Times. "The Nation: Focus Groups?; To Bush, the Crowd Was a Blur." Last updated February 23, 2003. Retrieved February 16, 2004. http://nytimes.com.

Robbins, Tom. Still Life with Woodpecker. New York: Bantam Books, 1980.

BIBLIOGRAPHY

Romano, Tricia. The Village Voice. "A Crash Course in Cabarets." Last modified November 26, 2002. Retrieved October 5, 2004. http://www.villagevoice.com.

Rubenstein, Jeff. "Purim, Liminality, Communitas." Association for Jewish Studies Review. 17. no. 2 (1992): p. 247-250.

Santos, Fernanda. New York Times. "Boisterous Protest Interrupts Bloomberg." Last modified February 3, 2009. Retrieved February 5, 2009. http://www.nytimes.com.

Savage, Charlie. New York Times. "Senators Say Patriot Act Is Being Misinterpreted." Last modified May 26, 2011. Retrieved September 8, 2011. http://www.nytimes.com.

Sawyer, Eric. "An ACT UP founder 'acts up' for Africa's access to AIDS." Edited by Ben Shepard and Ronald Hayduk. London and New York: Verso, 2002. p. 88-102.

Shechner, Richard. "The Street is the Stage." Radical Street Performances. Edited by Jan Cohen-Cruz. London and New York: Routledge, 1998.

Shepard, Ben and Ronald Hayduk. From ACT UP to the WTO Urban Protest and Community Building in the Era of Globalization. London and New York: Verso, 2002. p. 261.

Storey, John. Inventing Popular Culture: From Folklore to Globalization. Malden, MA: Blackwell Publishing, 2003. p. 49.

Walker, Hunter. Policker. "Mayor Bloomburg: 'I Have My Own Army.'" Retrieved January 8, 2012. http://www.politicker.com.

AUTHOR BIO

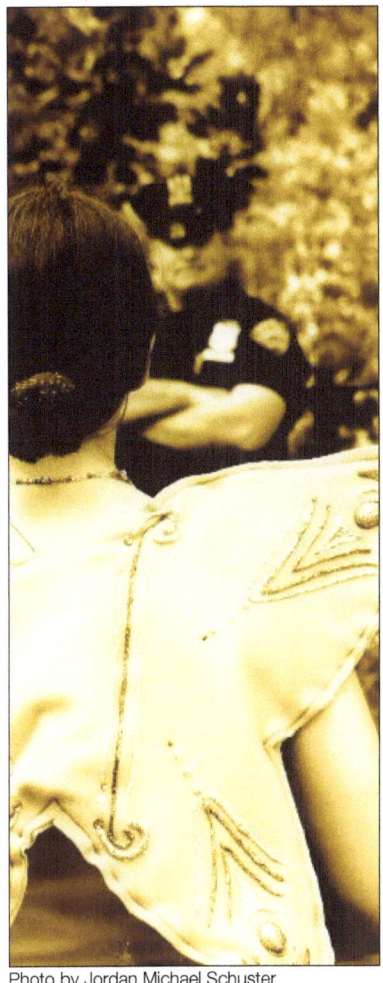

Photo by Jordan Michael Schuster

Sarah Sparkles is an interdisciplinary artist whose passions include photography, writing, teaching, jewelry design, accessories, costumes, prop building, installation art, and dance. Sarah graduated Magna Cum Laude from Purchase College in 2004 with a degree in Media, Society, and the Arts, and received the Mike McNickle Journalism Award for investigative reporting. In 2006, she assisted Donna Ferrato, an internationally acclaimed photojournalist and author of *Living with the Enemy*. Sarah was deeply influenced by Ferrato's use of photography as a medium for empowering her subjects and readers, for raising awareness, and implementing social justice.

Born and raised in New York, Sarah's love of expressive adornment, alternative communities and dance music inspired her to spend over a decade deeply immersed in NYC's underground nightlife subcultures. During this time, she participated as an avid costumer, performer, decor artist, door girl, and dance enthusiast, all the while documenting some of the party scene's most exuberant exploits as well as the visual art of the post-9/11 anti-war protest movements. Sarah became intensely driven by a desire to help this underrepresented transformative arts movement make its mark on history. The result is this book. 12 years in the making, *Parades, Parties, and Protests* is a bold tribute to the creative resistance culture of the 21st century.

For more information on Sarah's work, please visit her website at sarahsparkles.com.

CREDITS

Essays, photography, and poetry by Sarah Sparkles
Text edited by Sairica Rose, Pinky Weitzman, and Nick Bush
Chapter icons by Miko Graphics
Page design and graphic layout by Nick Bush
Cover design by Steve Pagan

ACKNOWLEDGEMENTS

My upmost gratitude and appreciation goes out to: My grandparents Rachel and Ralph Cooper for EVERYTHING, my creative team for your dedicated efforts in finalizing this book, additional support from Teagan Blackburn, Abby Hertz, Christian Soberanis, Rebecca Bullene, Robert Wrazen, and Ernesto Vallejo with refining text and/or graphic content, and my numerous patient and astute friends and colleagues who have given me solid feedback on the book content and advice on publishing over the years. I couldn't have done this without you.

Special thanks to all the NYC event producers and collectives who provided a platform for the dynamic alternative culture featured in this book: Sari from Rubulad, Winkel, Rhiannon and the rest of the Lunatarium crew, Missy Galore, Will Etundi from Complacent/the Danger and Arrow Chrome from Bio Tour/Blackkat. To all the brave visionary souls who are currently holding the torch, producing, and participating in avant-garde nightlife and arts culture in New York City and beyond, I salute you.

CREATIVE TEAM

Sairica Rose - sairica.com
Pinky Weitzman - pinkyweitzman.com
Michael "Miko" Bratland - mikographics.com
Nick Bush - decolimited.com
Steve Pagan - pagansoundsystem.com
Abby Hertz - ahzconcepts.com
Robert Wrazen - wrazen.com

FEATURED ARTISTS

– In order of appearance –

Amy Shapiro - amyshapiro.com - (p. 13)

Judy Sky - (p. 13)

Felix Ashara Chrome - (p. 18)

Ben Sheppard - benjaminheimshepard.com - (p. 30)

Machine Dazzle - imaginefashion.com/ladies-gentlemen/sacred-objects-machine-dazzle - (p. 36)

"Debbie" Despina Sophia Stamos - tmdas.org - (p. 36)

Missile Dick Chicks - missiledickchicks.net - (p. 36)

Rolando Politi - everydaytrash.com/tag/rolando-politi - (p. 44)

Chashama - chashama.org - (p. 48)

Earth Celebrations - earthcelebrations.com - (p. 53)

Jersey Walz - jerseywalzphotography.com - (p. 55)

Arrow Chrome - arrowchrome.com - (p. 62)

Rhiannon "Catalyst" Erbach - soundcloud.com/rhiannoncatalyst - (p. 62)

Scott Hopkins - standardsoundstudio.com - (p. 64)

Malcolm Stuart - malcolmstuart.com - (p. 67)

Whelan Dean-Ford - wheylan.com - (p. 67)

Chris "Flambeaux" Reilly - flambeauxfire.com & flambeauxfireeater.com - (p. 68)

Brite Lite - britelite.info/about.html - (p. 69)

Candice Vincent - (p. 69)

Stefan Pildes - stefanmakes.com & groovehoops.com - (p. 69)

Rudy Yardley - rudiyardley.com - (p. 70)

Darlinda Just Darlinda - darlindajustdarlinda.com - (p. 71)

Shamanatrix Missy Galore - fluffthegoodness.com & missygalore.com - (p. 84)

Will Etundi Jr. - thedanger.com - (p. 92)

Anya Sapozhnikova and Kae Burke - ladycircus.com & houseofyes.org - (p. 92)

Charlotte Lily Gaspard - cspotdesigns.blogspot.com - (p. 93)

Taylor Kuffner a.k.a. Zemi 17 - gamelatron.com & zemi17.net - (p. 94)

Fay Serafica - data23.blogspot.com - (p. 95)

Sandhi Ferreira - sandyoga.com & acromukti.com - (p. 97)

Veronica Varlow - dangerdame.com - (p. 106)

Dicie Carlson - (p. 106)